INNOCENCE & REALITY

A miraculous journey of faith and
family during WWII

Mathew E. Sikorski, Ph.D.

To

Deborah & Howard

with my best wishes

Mathew E. Sikorski, Ph.D.

Cover and Book design: Jessica Mitchem
Production: SPS Publications
www.spsbooks.com

Table of contents

Dedication

I dedicate this book to my beloved family, all of my friends and acquaintances, and all the compassionate people who commit themselves, in whatever capacity, to work for peace and justice in the world.

Acknowledgments

First, I would like to thank Almighty God for preserving and protecting me through the events of this book.

I want to thank my wife, Barbara, who has stood by me for 48 years. Her hard work and dedication in making a success of her sandwich shop, appropriately named by her, "The Best Sandwich," gave me the freedom to live in England for several years while I completed my life-long dream of a Ph.D. degree. I also appreciate very much her strong encouragement not to limit this book to stories of "a boy and his dog during WWII," but to also express a strong, positive message from my war experiences. I will always cherish the wedding anniversary weeks we spent at the Adventure Inn on Hilton Head Island, South Carolina, where, often, we worked on the income taxes!

My special thanks go to our son, Tom, for his indefatigable support and multifarious contributions in helping me bring this book to completion. He composed some sections from my dictation and others from his knowledge of the story.

Our second son, Mark, made a thorough review of the first manuscript. In his remarks, at the completion of this work he posed a daunting question, "How important was religion in your life?" Mark's question stimulated me to review all of my life's experiences in this light.

I expect our youngest son, Chris, who also loves me very much, to receive the publication of my book with his typical, happy smile saying, "I am glad that you finished!"

I would like to thank Andrzej Lewandowski and Aleksandra Hennig for being such good companions in my childhood days. I knew Andrzej since the days of being small enough for both of us to fit under a Christmas tree and observe the lights from below. Aleksandra became my neighbor soon after the Germans occupied Warsaw in September 1939 and was a great partner in a variety of sports and recreational activities.

I give special thanks to my close friend of many years, Joe Goldberg and his wife Patsy. I appreciate your unceasing encouragement to continue writing. Thank you, Joe, for contributing the Foreword for this book, being with me in North Georgia mountain cabins to finish the manuscript and for playing music with me. These are memories I will always cherish. I also admire your knowledge of computers!

My appreciation goes to Zbigniew Walczak for writing a section on the history of Poland, an abbreviated version of which was used in the Appendix.

I gratefully acknowledge reviews of the text by Bob Gutman, Joan Carroll, Susanne Dabney, Gwen

Robertson, Tom Sikorski and Dr. John Lundberg. I met my friend Dr. John Lundberg 45 years ago while we both worked at the Bell Telephone Laboratories in Murray Hill, New Jersey. Thank you, John, for offering me work on your research project at the time when I lost my own financial support during a re-organization at Georgia Tech.

John Evan, with whom my wife and I, at one time, sang in the church choir, took an early interest in my book and was helpful in many ways. Because of his avid interest in the history of WWII and his aid in putting a time line into the events described in my book, I like to call him the "official historian" of the work. Thank you John.

I am indebted to Sally Mc Donald, Joanne Kearney and Dick Bassett who were members with me of the Peace and Justice Committee at Our Lady of the Assumption Catholic Church in Atlanta, Georgia. They invited me to give the first public talks on my WWII experiences. You inspired me to follow the talks with a written account.

I am also indebted to Linda Clopton, who facilitated a writing workshop, which helped me immensely with my initial efforts to write this book. The essays I wrote later became chapters. The immediate feedback from my classmates was invaluable in developing the material.

I extend my appreciation to the people who are friends and colleagues in my ongoing quest for personal and spiritual growth. The Wednesday night Contemplative Prayer group includes: my wife, Barbara, Martha Doster, Barbara Moseley, Jose Blanco, Sherry Barnett, Faye Hickman, Jo Ponzillo, Bernardine Purcell, Gwen Robertson, Gianni West and Rita Sotomayor. Our Saturday noon group, which is called the late Fr. Ed Murray Workshop (based on the Twelve Step program), always provides new insights and community support. In addition to most of the above-mentioned people, Margie Simonoff, Chris Hume, Franci Etheridge, Katherine Baldwin, Peggy Hoeler and Sally McDonald were faithful members of this workshop, since its inception in 1992. Your friendship and support have made it possible for me to keep the dream alive of telling my story.

I am also indebted to Connie Dodge—Atlanta's foremost storyteller—who provided a special forum of avid listeners for my war stories during a course she taught at the Atlanta Arts Center. This opportunity helped me to get ready to try to motivate young people in their quest for a meaningful and happy life.

I am grateful for the inspiration in my spiritual growth given to me over the years by two television shows. They are: "The Hour of Power" by Dr. Robert Schuller and the "Oprah Winfrey Show." I have watched Robert Schuller for about 30 years and Oprah's "Life in the Spirit" shows, particularly when they were applicable to men.

And finally, I can never forget the veterans of the Second Armored Division of the 9th Army who liberated us and helped put an end to the bloodshed of WWII. It is unbelievable that after 58 years I met Dr. Morton Waitzman, who served in the American Infantry. They were the ones who freed the city of Hameln, including those in the forced labor camp where my mother and I worked. Of all places he lives in Atlanta, Georgia and occasionally shares the platform with me at the Breman Holocaust Museum where we share our stories!

Foreword

It is my pleasure to introduce my good friend Dr. Mathew Sikorski. We have spent many occasions discussing his story and even shared a mountain cabin while we both developed ideas for our books. This work describes his miraculous journey through a series of unforgettable experiences.

As a youth, Mathew's physical limitations did not allow him to contend in the sparing boys often engage in. He had to learn how to survive without violence, yet remain courageous.

People in our society go on and on about how our children must be protected from any kind of trauma, minor or major, while others have had experiences that practically no young person alive in America today can begin to imagine. Yet, many like Mathew finish school, get married, raise a family, have careers, belong to a church and stay out of trouble – all the things we revere in this country. Can we say the same about our over-protected youth? He was supportive of his family in times of difficulty, unlike many people who rush to divorce.

Mathew is a delightful, warm individual, with a good sense of humor, who, for the past decade has grown emotionally and spiritually. He is involved in self-help groups, church ministries, reading, music, speaking and learning about many things. How many seventy-three-year-olds can say the same thing? In retirement Mathew has had the opportunity to experience the camaraderie of other men and delight in their acceptance of him as a brave and progressive man. He is a model for many. In this writing, you will read about the real Mathew Sikorski, as he takes life on its own terms, one step at a time, holding no grudges and with a zest that rarely dims.

As his experiences unfold before your imagination, you will wonder how you would have handled each situation, how you would have come through. Could I have endured the loss of a comfortable life, torn out at its roots and succeeded in another culture on the other side of the world? Or, in the words of a country-western song, would I have folded and left the game?

Joe P. Goldberg
1933-2003

Preface

The purpose of my book is to share with the reader my feelings of enchantment about life and to motivate young people to strive for the fulfillment of their God-given potential. I found such a journey to be very rewarding. What a joy it has been to be able to constantly observe, learn and experience the different manifestations of life – spiritual, as well as material. From the perspective of over 70 years, I see the handiwork of my Creator in everything that happened to me, particularly from age ten to sixteen during the Second World War. In spite of often finding myself in great danger, I was able to survive the war, thanks to God's grace.

I started sheepishly describing my wartime experiences to my friends only a few years ago. Since the end of WWII, memories of different events kept coming back over and over, year after year, day and night. Initially, I had no thought or intention of writing a book. However, after being invited to talk on the subject twice, the videotaping of one of the talks by my son, Tom, and repeated requests for copies of the tape, I decided to put my memories on paper.

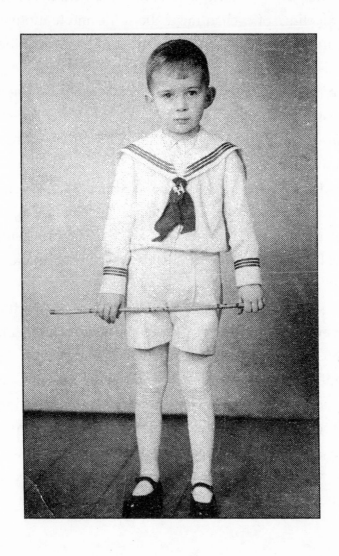

The early days

I was born in Warsaw, Poland on March 20th, 1929. I was a blue baby, since my heart was malformed. The defect could not be diagnosed at the time, except for the doctor's stethoscope detecting a strong murmur.

When I was four years old, I remember one specific visit to the doctor with both of my parents, which turned out to be a very traumatic experience. I remember the scene vividly: I was propped up on the edge of the examination table in the doctor's office and he listened to my heart. He did not say anything to me, but asked my parents to go to another room with him. They were not talking very loudly, yet I was still able to hear part of the conversation. He essentially encouraged them to have another child, because he believed I would not survive until my tenth birthday due to the severity of my heart defect. This statement surprised me because I felt okay.

When I started going to school at age six, there was a girl in my class named Basia (a diminutive for Barbara) whom I found very attractive. She had long, braided, dark blonde hair. I liked her so much I started praying to God that when I fell asleep, I would wake up looking just like her. I prayed very earnestly for this wish for some time. God answered "no" and to my dismay I had to remain just as I was.

Wanting to appeal to the girls in my class, every morning before school, I would use my mother's curling iron to put a loop in the short hair over my forehead. My parents never objected to this practice. Since I was an only child and one not expected to live very long, they did not want to interfere with my creativity!

As was the custom for Catholic boys my age, the day came to see a priest about becoming an altar boy. I was shocked to find that the stern man did not appreciate my attempt to have a stylish hair-do. He angrily grabbed my hand, led me to a sink and washed my hair to remove the curl. I was terribly upset and promptly told my mother what had happened. The result was, I never became an altar server. I think that this was a shame, because the experience of being in the front of the church each Sunday may have helped me overcome the shyness with which I have struggled all my life.

One of the great joys of my childhood was going with my grandfather, just before Christmas, to Ogród Saski (Saski Gardens), a park in the middle of the city of Warsaw. When we arrived, it was our custom to stop and enjoy a matzo wafer, made of unleavened bread, purchased from an elderly woman street vendor. We would then select and take home a large Christmas tree at least six feet tall. At home I would decorate the tree with a large number of multi-colored electric lights, tiny red apples, candy and paper chains consisting of links made of different colors of crêpe paper. The tree was more than twice my size, since the ceiling in our apartment was close to eleven feet high.

Another favorite holiday tradition was going to visit my aunt and uncle who lived about a thirty-minute walk from our apartment. My Aunt Fela would always have a special plate of faworki (deep-fried crepe strips covered with powdered sugar) hidden for me in the cupboard. They were so good that she had to keep them hidden until I arrived, so her sons would not eat them first!

We also enjoyed visiting my Grandmother Franciszka (Frances) on my father's side. She lived near the Vistula River. She liked to make cherry whiskey by filling a huge glass jar with large, dark red cherries and covering them with sugar. The cherries would ferment and make a delightful drink indeed! Being too young to drink, I got to eat some of the cherries, instead.

At my Uncle Stanislaw's (Stanley's) house there was a marble mantelpiece over his fireplace. Standing upon it was a large replica, about one foot-long, of a dark green Mercedes-Benz sports car, which was made in Germany. My uncle would often let me play with this car. I was fascinated by the doors and hood, which could be opened. When the doors were shut they sounded just like the doors of a real car. The wheels could be turned with the steering wheel. I was amused for hours just examining the details on that car and admiring the precision with which it was made.

On another visit, the son of one of the guests had a horseshoe-shaped magnet. I wanted to have it so badly that he agreed to give me half. As much as both of us, and some of the adults present tried, we could not break it apart. I did not realize, at the time, that had we succeeded, it would not have worked anymore since the North and South poles would not be close enough to generate a strong magnetic field between them. This experience stuck in my memory as I would, perhaps five years later, get my own magnets, although much smaller ones, and use them to operate puppets in a theater I built to amuse my friends. All I had to do was to glue a thin sheet of metal, which could be attracted by a magnet, to the bottom of the puppet. The puppet would move on stage, which was made of plywood, by a magnet I held underneath the floor, hidden from the spectators. Some children thought that I was a magician!

In Poland, on the Monday after Easter it is customary for boys to play practical jokes on girls, which involve sprinkling water or perfume on them. This custom is known as "Śmigus Dyngus." Once I took full advantage of this opportunity to have some fun. From my third story window, I used my bicycle pump as a high-powered squirt gun to soak the ladies walking below. In the countryside, the water play was often a bit more aggressive with men catching young women and dunking them into a barrel of water!

Like all good parents, mine wanted me to be exposed to things that would make me a well-rounded person. They hired a piano teacher who, unfortunately, wanted me to practice scales rather than the songs I wanted to sing. Seven years of private lessons paid off, however, since I can still play anything by ear. My mother and father hoped I would continue to develop my voice as well, until, unfortunately, puberty robbed me of my melodious tone.

When I was about ten my father hired an art teacher to come to our house and give drawing lessons to some of his interested employees and me. This was a way to not only learn another form of self-expression, but also a way of being included in the continuing education he so fervently believed in. I remember making a drawing, which showed railroad tracks disappearing in the distance. This taught me about perspective.

My mother contributed to my cultural exposure by taking me to a place called the Cyclorama. There we observed three-dimensional pictures of scenes from other countries. I was fascinated by the differences in the way people looked in different parts of the world.

Another museum we visited featured a display of a developing fetus in the mother's womb. What I wanted to know was how it got in there in the first place! My father felt that I was too young to be told anything more than the commonly propagated story of the stork. Thus, I had to learn the truth from my friends.

One day my father took me to an arena to see a boxing match. I enjoyed having the opportunity to watch this event with him. My mother, on the other hand, was most distressed that I had witnessed first-hand such a brutal sport.

Like most people, my favorite family memories were of our vacations. A visit to my uncle's farm provided me the opportunity to learn to ride both a bike and a horse.

Poland is blessed with beautiful mountains and one of our favorite places to visit was called Krynica. At the very top of the mountain I would lie on my stomach and enjoy the majestic scenery while eating the huge, luscious blackberries without the use of my hands.

Zakopane is a ski resort town in the Carpathian Mountains, on the border of Czechoslovakia, now the Czech Republic and Slovakia. It was here that my family rode a cable car to the top of the mountain, which is called "Kasprowy Vierch." It was winter and from there we skied down the mountain using a "Nartostrada," or man-made ski run, which was full of surprises in the form of sudden turns and steep slopes. For someone who was supposed to be in as fragile health as I was, it was amazing how active I was allowed to be. My favorite part of this trip was watching my mother sail off an icy ledge into a deep puddle of ice-cold water! She forgot to bend her knees and fell forward like a tree that had been chopped off!

Quiet before the storm

Our last vacation far away from Warsaw was the month we rented a room on the Baltic Sea. My father was able to leave his business for a week to join us. There, he organized a game of "palant," which is similar to baseball, for the boys who were in the area at the time. I felt very hurt that he did not want me to participate; perhaps he felt it would be too much of a strain on my heart.

I enjoyed looking for amber stones on the beach and watching the fishermen catch eels. Taking out a wooden rowboat gave me the chance to observe jellyfish. They glistened in the water, undulating with a breath-like motion. Some were pale pink, some blue and others green, but they all looked the same - gelatinous; transparent, and seemingly devoid of life when I scooped them out of the water with a fisherman's net for a closer look. What an intriguing place this was!

On the way back to Warsaw, we took a train to the cities of Gdynia and Gdańsk. Gdynia was a rather new city with wide streets and white/gray buildings. [Gdańsk looked ancient in comparison, its history dating back to the year 1000 A.D., almost as old as the country of Poland, whose history began in the year 996 A.D.] What struck me as very odd was that Gdańsk, the city which was supposed to be "free," that is, have equal access by Poles and Germans alike, at the end of WWI as agreed upon by the peace agreement, was almost completely colonized by the Germans. The Polish language could not be heard in the streets and seemingly all the streets carried German names. The language used in stores was also German. As history shows, the Germans were at that time already preparing for the invasion of Poland, which took place on September 1, 1939, thus starting WWII. Gdańsk was attacked from the sea on the same day.

From Gdansk, my parents and I took an overnight train to return to Warsaw. At midnight the train stopped in Toruń, the birthplace of Polish astronomer, Nicolaus Copernicus. Today, Toruń has the largest astronomical laboratory in Poland. I happened to be awake at the time and as soon as the train stopped, I heard the yells of the vendors, "Pierniczki Toruńskie," or gingerbread honey cookies from Toruń. My mother opened the window of the sleeper car and bought me a bag of these heart-shaped, chocolate-covered, delicious cookies. I must have liked them well enough, along with the excitement associated with a train ride and not sleeping at midnight, that I remember the event to this day.

As the sun set on our seaside vacation, little did I know that this was the end of the peaceful, colorful and joyful family life I had always known.

The small voice

It was the beginning of September 1939. I was ten years old, and still an only child. In spite of frequent pleading with my parents to provide me with a sister or a brother, it seemed that they were not doing anything to satisfy my wishes. The city of Warsaw, Poland, was under siege by the German Army and the Polish Army was retreating from the Western Front.

During the first few days of the war, we saw hundreds and hundreds of people of all ages walk by our third story apartment windows on Krakowskie Przedmieście (Cracow's Suburb) Street, or ride in horse-drawn carriages, trying to escape the onslaught of German forces. The exodus stopped once the German troops started to storm Warsaw.

One week went by peacefully for my family. In spite of frequent bombing and artillery shelling of the city, I was not aware of any damage to the adjoining houses. At night we kept only a few lights on in our apartment, even though all of the windows were completely covered with black cardboard. We did this to avoid being seen which could invite disaster in form of a bomb or artillery shell.

I remember standing with my back toward the balcony and looking into the room. My mother was to my left and my father to my right. Behind mother was my parents' double bed. In the back and somewhat to the right of my father was my mother's beautiful dresser with three oval mirrors. The French-style dresser contained a large, tall, central mirror. The contour of the wooden frame on top followed its gentle curve. The mirror was permanently attached to the base of the dresser. The other two mirrors, located on each side of the center one, could be rotated in any position with the help of vertical hinges, to allow viewing of the sides of the head while sitting on a stool in front of the dresser. The stool was also oval-shaped. It was well padded for softness and was covered with an attractive white and gold fabric. The base of the dresser was sufficiently wide so that all three mirrors were located above it. Normally, there was a bottle or two of perfume, or eau de cologne, sitting on top of the dresser. The bottles were very pretty, made out of cut crystal glass. The bottle of eau de Cologne had a flexible tube and a rubber bulb attached to it. The bulb was covered with a yellow net-like fabric. The dresser also featured a number of shelves in three rows with round, shiny brass knobs.

I loved to watch my mother, who was of medium build and very pretty, fix her hair while seated in front of the dresser. A discrete light, supported by a gold-colored, horizontal, cylindrical support was attached to the frame of the dresser just above the central mirror. It provided all the necessary illumination for a fine make-up job. The construction and position of the light were similar to those normally used to illuminate pictures in art galleries.

Her make-up would normally take longer than usual before my parents were about to go to a dance. This usually happened just before Advent and Lent in honor of the period of preparation for the solemn religious celebrations of Christ's birth, death and resurrection. Although I would have to fall asleep all by myself on such occasions, without first listening to bedtime stories read by my mother, I had the assurance that there would be beautiful, colorful, helium-filled balloons attached to the frame of my bed when I awakened the following morning. I was a real tyrant as far as mother's attention was concerned; however, the anticipation of having the balloons to play with was well worth the bargain!

The finish on all the furniture in the master bedroom was of a beautiful light oak. Besides the bed and the dresser, there was also a wardrobe set against the back wall and an ottoman located in an adjoining alcove where my father used to take his siesta or an after-lunch nap. Just like the dresser, other pieces of furniture in this room are associated with wonderful childhood memories.

The stand-alone wooden wardrobe was very large, like a walk-in closet and also quite tall. It featured sliding doors for easy access to the interior. The brick-and-concrete walls in our apartment did not allow for clothes racks to be built into walls as is common in America, where plasterboard is commonly used for home construction. The cost of re-modeling would have been astronomical.

The structure of the wardrobe case was sufficiently strong enough for me to climb, with the help of a small ladder. I liked to sit on top of it as a pretend observation tower. From this vantage point, I was often able to observe my dog and cat chase each other and play unnoticed in an area between my mother's side of the bed and the balcony. Climbing on top of the wardrobe case would not have been possible were it not for the fact that the ceilings were eleven feet high in our apartment. This was the standard ceiling height in buildings constructed at the end of the 19th century in the historical part of Warsaw where we lived. Even now, I still have a preference for houses with rooms having high ceilings.

Between the wardrobe and my father's side of the bed was a pretty red–and-blue oriental throw rug. My father enjoyed stepping on this runner, rather than on the cold, hardwood floor, when he arose from bed each morning. Early one day, I overheard from my adjoining bedroom, an animated conversation between my parents. I became curious what was going on, so I knocked on the door between my bedroom and theirs, and entered the room. It turned out that my beloved dog, Miki, the third Chihuahua dog that I owned, happened to have confused my father's bedside carpet for his sand box that morning. I proceeded to explain to my father that this type of dog has a very small brain and such accidents are likely to happen. My mother broke in and said, "We haven't owned Miki very long; we'll spend more time in the future training him."

The sofa was located in an alcove on the side of the bedroom. It was the site of one of my biggest joys in childhood. As soon as my father lay down on the sofa and covered himself with his jacket, my little Chihuahua dog darted onto the sofa, barely able to make it because of his small size. He then nosed his way under the jacket to sleep in my father's right armpit, for as long as the siesta lasted, which was usually about twenty minutes. I loved to watch them go through this ritual every day.

Despite growing unrest outside our home, my parents were surprisingly calm. They did not seem to be afraid of staying in our apartment during the night, in spite of the fact that air-raid sirens would often blare and many of our neighbors went to their cellars night after night.

I remember vividly, even though more than 60 years have passed, how my parents' bedroom looked and where we stood when, one afternoon, my father slowly uttered, "I think that we ought to go to the cellar tonight." My mother and I promptly agreed, although his suggestion seemed sudden.

Before it got dark we went to the basement loaded with blankets and pillows in our hands. We had to clear off and prepare some floor space to be able to lie down for the night.

Most of the floor in the cellar was normally covered with coal at the end of the summer for heating our apartment during the long winter season. Heating of the apartment consisted of starting a fire in the combustion chambers of wall ovens. We had two such ovens in our ten-room apartment. One was located in the commercial section of the apartment (my father had a tailoring business) and the other in the living quarters. We also used space heaters.

The most difficult part of having large area wall ovens was the starting the fire around six o'clock in the morning in order to have a comfortable temperature by eight o'clock when my father's employees were expected to come to work. My mother was sometimes "elected" to perform the above chore. However, whenever possible, it was the job of our live-in maid.

The night in the cellar was uneventful and we were able to get some rest. There was no need to hurry to go back upstairs because my father's employees were not expected to come to work after the siege of Warsaw had begun. However, I felt like having breakfast and wanted to check on my toys upstairs.

I was ahead of my parents on the way up to the apartment. We had to climb two flights of stairs. I liked those stairs. They were made of wrought iron and were very tastefully ornamented. A peculiar resonant sound was given off by the structure when someone was climbing them. That sound, for me, was strangely energizing.

When I reached the top of the stairs I pulled out my key and opened the door. I entered through the business entrance to our apartment. My first thought was to go to the kitchen for a drink of water. First, I walked through a hallway to the clients' waiting room. Then, I opened the door to my bedroom, quickly checked whether all my toys were okay, and opened the door to my parents' bedroom.

I could not believe what I saw! I did not dare to enter that room without them being near. Fortunately, they were not far behind.

During the night a field artillery projectile had entered our apartment from the street, made a large hole in the external wall of the building, flown across the room where my father's tailors normally worked, pierced an additional wall, soared across a walk-in closet, went through another wall and finally exploded in my parents' bedroom.

When I opened the door, I saw everything covered

with a thick layer of dust. My nostrils became irritated by a very powerful odor of spent ammunition powder and what smelled like charred wood. I also acquired a taste of ash in my mouth. By that time, my parents had caught up with me and we all went silent at what we saw. The magnitude of the destruction caused by the explosion was unbelievable! My parents' bed was covered with chunks of metal of different sizes and shapes. The headboard was strewn with shrapnel. If we had not gone to the cellar that night, my parents would have been killed instantly and I would have become an orphan at age ten.

The rest of the room was also in shambles. My mother's three-mirror dresser that I had particularly liked was no more. It was located directly under the area of the wall where the projectile had entered the bedroom. The wardrobe was in pieces and the sofa on which my father used to take a siesta every day after lunch had disappeared completely.

I was certainly blessed by God to allow me to be cared for by my beloved parents for as long as it was possible. I have often wondered why this particular memory had been so deeply engrained in my brain. I have come to the conclusion that what happened carries a very profound message for me: my father managed to keep his life in balance and thus was able to hear, accept and surrender his will to the prompting of the small voice of intuition which saved my parents' lives.

Life goes on

Day by day, life began to change after the surrender of Warsaw. This event marked the beginning of the tragic years of occupation, which would be fraught with great hardships for the Poles. Almost immediately, the German occupation forces began to take control of the freedom we once knew. The officials of the Polish Government, who did not manage to escape the country, as well as distinguished university professors and many other members of the intelligentsia were rounded up, put in jail and executed, or put in labor or concentration camps. On the personal level, the German authorities ordered everyone, under the threat of capital punishment, to turn in any radios they had. We surrendered an old crystal radio, but hid in the attic a newer, vacuum tube one, which we never got to use.

The ideology of the Third Reich was that Slavs - hence also the Poles - were an inferior race and as such were not permitted to pursue a high school education. Trade schools, however, were allowed. Therefore, the principal of the Zamoyski's High School, where I was registered, decided to carry out educational activities under the guise that students were learning how to become fishermen. A large building in the city was rented for the avowed establishment of what was called "The School of Fisheries." Initially, the students brought their textbooks to school. They were told to immediately hide the books in the desk drawer if an inspector should come. The walls of the classrooms had pictures of different kinds of fish. I remember those days as being rather unnerving. There was always the threat that we could be discovered and severely punished by the German occupiers. There was a close call one day and the teachers decided to abandon this scheme. It was decided that, instead, we would meet with the teacher in small groups of students in private homes every day. We had to keep moving the location of the clandestine meeting so as not to attract anyone's attention. That is how I attended high school until the Warsaw Uprising on August 1, 1944.

We did not know this at the time, but the conditions in Poland were different from and considerably harsher than those experienced by citizens in Western European countries. Along with the Jews, peoples of the occupied countries of Central and Eastern Europe would also have been completely annihilated had Hitler been victorious. The Nuremberg Trials showed that the Nazis had formulated a plan for the occupied territories east of Germany for after the war. According to this plan, fifty million Slavs were to have been forcibly resettled in Siberia after the German victory over the Soviet Union. This number included about twenty million Poles, with complete elimination of the

Polish intelligentsia. The Germans were methodically carrying out this plan.

A few months after the fall of Warsaw, Jewish people were required to wear a Star of David emblem on their outer garments for purposes of identification. This allowed the German soldiers to require that Jews step off the pavement onto the street when they saw a German approaching them. The next step in the persecution, which was obvious to most inhabitants of Warsaw, was to start the construction of the Jewish ghetto in a designated part of the city. The entire Jewish population of Warsaw was eventually moved to the ghetto. In addition, those who lived in some outlying areas were also taken to the Warsaw ghetto. Larger towns had their own ghettos. Eventually, practically all the Jews from Poland were taken to concentration camps for eventual extermination. The Germans planned and executed their strategy with such perfection that no one was able to suspect the worst scenario. There was no detectable threshold of abuse at which people could say no, and then revolt in some fashion!

My family tried to maintain some semblance of normalcy in everyday life. We continued to go on picnics on Sundays, as often as we could, to a forest in a little town called Bielany. These were one-day trips, because the use of streetcars was the preferred mode of travel. It took about one and a half hours to get there.

If it rained before we got there, I enjoyed looking for mushrooms in the forest; otherwise, there wasn't much to do there. The trick with mushrooms was to know which ones were poisonous and which ones weren't. Upon our return home, as soon as we entered the back yard, I was always thrilled to see my dog and cat sitting on the edge of the balcony, which was located off of my parents' bedroom. When we opened the entrance door to our apartment, the scene was always the same: my dog was incredibly excited to see us return, barking and jumping up-and-down until I picked him up. The cat, as usual, would run away! My female Siamese cat, Kizia, detested my touching her. If I managed to touch her, she would lick herself for hours, infuriating me to no end.

In the winter I liked to ice skate in a skating rink, which was located fairly close to my house. Since the only skates I had were the kind that attached to my shoes, I dreamed that someday I might have real shoe skates to be able to do some figure skating, or even better, racing skates with a sharp edge.

I also had a sled, which was large enough for four of my friends to ride with me. I had to use my right foot, which had a skate on it, to steer our sled as we raced down the hill. One time, my friends and I were nearly killed as we went so fast on the sheer, ice-covered surface of a steep incline, that we crossed the street right in front of an approaching German troop carrier loaded with soldiers. If we had arrived a few seconds later, we would have plowed into it. My parents never heard this story!

One evening, I brought my big sled into the kitchen and tried to support it against the wall with my left hand while groping for the electrical switch with my right. As was normally the case, Miki always ran into the room when he heard someone coming in the door. He would greet us by jumping up and down until he was picked up off the floor. He loved to lick me thoroughly, but not on this occasion. Before I managed to turn on the electricity, the sled slipped from my hand and fell on the floor with a loud thud. When the light came on I could see that the impossible had happened. As the sled fell, it hit Miki on the head, killing him instantly. My mother and I cried and cried for days. I stopped crying when my parents promised to get another dog for me. I just hoped that it would have a larger brain than Miki's.

As time went on, I discovered that I had a knack for mechanical things. This included repairing my father's sewing machines and fixing any electrical problems in our apartment. I liked to play with wind-up propeller planes in a nearby field. In the stores, I could buy pre-printed cardboard sheets, which could be cut out and glued together to make the buildings of a miniature city. I must have had infinite patience to do this! Not satisfied to stop there, I also wired my little town with electric lights. To add some pizzazz to the scene, I glued together a paper airplane that could fly over the city suspended on a long stretch of sewing thread spanning the room. I hoped that, someday, my father would get me an electric train rather than my old wind-up one. Tragedy struck when the gear in the locomotive wore out and a replacement could not be purchased. I sought out a machine shop in my neighborhood hoping that a new gear could be manufactured there, but the mechanic did not have the right kind of steel to attempt to do it. I was devastated! These interests seem to have foreshadowed the work I would do with scientific instrumentation for the rest of my professional life.

While we were trying to carry on, city life was getting frightening. One day our family was walking down the street and a man who passed us whispered to my father, "roundup," which was a warning that in the direction he was coming from, German soldiers were catching people and carrying them away to be put in a concentration camp, or sent to Germany for forced labor. We immediately changed direction, grateful that once again we had escaped harm.

Starting around the year 1943, approximately coinciding with the German effort to take the remaining Jewish population from the Warsaw ghetto to concentration camps, new tactics against the non-Jewish, or Christian population of Warsaw were started by the Germans. This was to sow terror in the hearts of the people. Large and very powerful loudspeakers were installed on lampposts all over the city. In the mornings, a number of adult males were caught in the streets while walking to work and then, ten at a time were executed in the afternoons by firing squads in different streets of the city. It was very frightening to walk in the streets of Warsaw and listen to the names of future victims of execution as they were announced. Since no one was allowed to have radios, this was the only available means of communication, in addition to posters that appeared from time to time across the city. It could have been my father, or some other member of my family! Of course, every man who lived in the city was a member of someone's family. One day I happened to have had a close call, myself, and I will talk about it in the next chapter.

A very important part of coping with the growing uncertainty about the future during the war was the solace provided by the Catholic Church. Not only were the Mass and other prayer services a constant in our lives, but also, people were unified, informed and given hope from the pulpit.

Not an ordinary day

It was a beautiful day in the spring of 1943. I was 14 and enjoying the break in the weather. Birds were singing, and leaves were coming out on every tree. It appeared to be the end of a harsh winter.

The only nagging thought in my mind on that day was how my father would react to my charring a one-by-one foot area of the floor in one of the rooms in our apartment during my childhood war games. Granted, the wooden floor in this room was not as shiny and polished as in the rest of our apartment, but still, it was the workroom of men who were employed by my father.

I always tried to be very cautious in my endeavors, but this time I goofed. One of the paper houses of the city that I built on the floor caught on fire, as a result of the use of my ingenious flame-thrower, which used a flammable liquid, acetone. Before I had a chance to extinguish it by running through five rooms to the kitchen for water, the floor was discolored. My mother was not too happy about this "accident," and I wondered what my father's reaction would be. He was out of town that day and was expected to return home that very night.

Right after lunch I climbed on my bike and proceeded to visit my tutor for another German lesson. It was customary for me, in those days, to study German and English every Tuesday and Thursday. My parents thought there was a good chance I might need to know foreign languages in the future. Normally, I would have enrolled in foreign languages in high school; however, the German authorities, which considered Poles to be an inferior race, did not allow higher education in Poland. All high schools were officially closed at the start of the German occupation in September of 1939.

My bike ride to see my teacher that afternoon was uneventful; however, my return home was not quite so ordinary! I took Miodowa Street, which was about two miles from my house. When I began to smell smoke, my curiosity was aroused about where the odor was coming from. I didn't have to wait long to find out!

I went around a curve and found myself on the opposite side of the wall from the Warsaw ghetto. All of the buildings I could see inside were in flames. My heart went out to the people, who were now subjected to, perhaps, the worst form of persecution imaginable; namely, to be burned alive. I found out after the war that only ten persons escaped from the ghetto in May 1943 through city sewers into the ethnic Polish part of town, and survived the war with the help of compassionate people who lived on the other side of the wall.

I slowed down and watched in horror as the flames blew out windows. Broken glass cascaded down the side of the building. The crackling of the fire was tremendous! Cinders were spewing out into the street and the smoke was starting to irritate my nostrils. I could even taste ash in my mouth. I heard sporadic rifle fire and short bursts from machine guns behind the wall. I also recall that some of the rifle fire was coming from tall buildings on the opposite side of Miodowa Street and was directed into the ghetto. Snipers must have had a good view of the area between the buildings that were on fire.

Although the outside walls of buildings were made out of stone and brick, the inside construction consisted only of wood. Whoever was able to flee the inferno did not have much time, if any, to gather up his or her belongings.

I could only see the top two or three floors of the buildings closest to the street because the wall surrounding the ghetto was about ten to twelve feet high. Because of this I was spared the view of the tragedy taking place on the ground behind the wall!

Suddenly, I saw in the smoke what appeared to be a silhouette of a man running, first visible through one window opening and then another. Then the image disappeared. Perhaps the burning floor gave way under his feet.

The first thought I had when the man's silhouette disappeared from view was what might have happened to my benefactor, the man whom I had never met and who, two years earlier, had donated his son's movie projector to my father for me to play with. He anticipated how much this movie projector would mean to me when he was giving it away. This man knew I would put it to good use.

This gesture was also a good-bye present for my father (through me) because, as he explained to my father, he would no longer be able to work with him by supplying buttons, sewing thread and other tailoring paraphernalia. He and his family were told by the German occupation authorities that because they were Jewish they would have to move to another part of Warsaw to live in an area especially designated for the Jews. As it turned out, it was a walled-in part of town, namely, the ghetto.

As I took another turn down Miodowa Street and proceeded in the direction of home, a thought came to my mind that probably the same fate would meet the rest of the people of Warsaw.

As I was nearing the next intersection, that of Miodowa Street with Senatorska Street, I suddenly realized that all of the pedestrians on both sides of the street were not walking any more, but actually running away from the intersection I was approaching. There was no way for me to ask anybody why they were running. It was clear that whatever was happening probably wasn't good! I soon found out!

Five German soldiers stood in a line, raising their carbines in the westerly direction of Senatorska Street, which is at right angles to Miodowa Street. None of the soldiers appeared to be looking in my direction. What should I do? I saw only two choices: one, to turn my bike around in full view of the soldiers, and take the risk of being shot in the back, or to brave them and quickly appear in front of their noses. I thought that turning my bike around would take too much time and I would chance being noticed; therefore, I decided to apply an element of surprise. I pumped my bike hard, and with a loud screech stopped in front of the soldier in the middle, just in front of the muzzle of his raised carbine. Using my newly acquired knowledge of German I yelled out, "What do you want me to do?" He responded with one word, "Raus!" (Get lost!) Obviously, this was exactly what I wanted to do!

I don't think I ever pedaled my bike harder, or ever will!

Seconds later I heard a furious volley of bullets punishing those who dared to be in Senatorska Street on that beautiful spring afternoon.

Concerning the punishment by my father for charring the floor of our apartment - there was none, he was so thankful that I had returned home alive!

The bullet was meant for me

There was fun wherever I looked. An orchard containing rows of strawberries, apple and cherry trees was at my disposal. I didn't relish anything more in the summer of 1944 than to be sitting in a tree and eating a cherry without having to wash it first. Besides, there were plenty of trees to climb and tree houses to build. There was a river for fishing. I hoped that some day a big fish would bite the bait. A plentiful supply of night crawlers enhanced my expectations. The farmhouse was also the place where I smoked my first cigar. I gathered two other fellows, in order to not be solely responsible for smoking, and we made cigars by rolling up large leaves from a maple tree. All was well until I inhaled. This was the last time I have ever tried to smoke!

Each year in the early 1940's I spent a month vacationing with my mother in a little town on the outskirts of the city of Warsaw called Józefów. My mother was able to rent a room for us, year after year, in a farmhouse, which was located close to a small river called Świder. The main attraction of this location was its close proximity to our home in Warsaw. It would have been very dangerous to travel far from home during the German occupation of Poland. Second, it constituted a virtual paradise for me, as a fifteen year old youngster.

It took one week to make myself stilts and two weeks

to learn how to stay in the air long enough to take the next step. I remember how determined I was to learn. I practiced every day, from first thing in the morning, until I couldn't do it any longer. Finally, the efforts paid off and I was able to cross a stream without getting wet. This was not an easy task. The water wasn't deep and it didn't offer much resistance to the motion of the stilts; however, the sand on the bottom was very soft in places and easily yielded to pressure. In order not to fall, it was necessary to quickly withdraw the stilt and put it down again in a nearby spot. This procedure was tiring, but well worth the effort.

It was time to go home and tell mother that I was able to cross the stream. I laid my stilts against the house near the entrance door and was about to enter when I saw a large cloud of dust behind a speeding car on the road leading to our house. In a few moments I was able to recognize that the car was actually a taxicab. A minute or two later the cab had stopped and the driver yelled out to me, "Where is your mother? Go and get her quickly. I'm taking you to Warsaw right now. If you do not hurry, I'll take somebody else." He subsequently jumped out of the taxi and pushed himself into the house to help carry out our bags.

After about an hour-and-a-half of a fast ride to Warsaw, the taxi driver dropped us off in front of our house and said, "Good luck, let God be with you."

The day was July 31, 1944. My father was standing at the door, anxiously awaiting our return. The first thing he said was, "I brought you back from your vacation because the uprising against the Germans is to start tomorrow morning." I recall having a queasy feeling in my stomach when I heard this news. I wasn't too happy about it, remembering the destruction of my parents' bedroom furniture during the siege of Warsaw and the horror of seeing the ghetto on fire a year before. It was also a close call for me not to have been killed in the street.

On the other hand, I remembered having experienced an air of excitement just prior to my vacation when my father told me that he had received an order to tailor a festive garment for a Polish Army officer. It was to be used during the victory parade after the defeat of the German forces in a carefully planned uprising. At that time, the Russian Army was pushing the Germans back and was expected to arrive on the outskirts of Warsaw during the summer.

The zero hour arrived. On the morning of August 1, 1944, I walked over to the window facing the street and I saw no pedestrians or vehicles anywhere. There was only ominous silence.

My parents were checking food supplies in our pantry. We had no idea as to how long the uprising might last. What we had was about 500 chicken eggs, two loaves of bread and 60 bottles of delicious French Sauterne wine. In those days, some clients would pay my father for his services with food rather than money. It was, of course, too late to buy supplies.

That afternoon I thought I'd re-check the scene in the street. I looked out the window and saw a man lying motionless on the pavement about three quarters of the way across the street. Somebody had shot him, and obviously there was no one to pull him away from the street. It was a scary sight. I had never seen a dead man in the street before. Since there was nothing I could do, I went back to the living quarters in the apartment.

On the following day, late in the afternoon, I went back to the front window to check on the man in the street. What I saw horrified me because some heavy vehicles must have ridden over his body during the night.

An instant later I heard the earsplitting sound of breaking glass, followed by silence. I instinctively closed my eyes. When I opened them again, I could see that the window glass in front of me was gone. Turning my head away from the window, I saw the bullet that was meant for me, stuck at the level of my eyes, in the concrete wall next to the window frame. I shuddered to the core.

That was the last time that I ever set foot in that room. By then, there was no doubt in my mind that the uprising had begun in earnest.

Exodus from Warsaw

The next morning, I woke up with a feeling of dread and loss of freedom. Because of the start of the uprising against the Germans and what I had gone through the previous afternoon, I was no longer free to take out my bike and enjoy a ride along the west bank of the Vistula river.

I could no longer go for a walk with my little Chihuahua dog, Enia. Of course, he would have to check out every little tree, and other objects that stuck out from the ground, like large stones and garbage cans. Unfortunately, we might be seen by someone with a rifle and never return home.

Neither could I just go out into the back yard for the heck of it. This was the place where I played ball with the girls. However, doing this earned me the nickname, "King of the Girls." (I was afraid to arrange games with the boys for fear of being beaten up), flew my numerous airplanes powered by twisted rubber bands, and in the winter months, skied down a hill or skated on a flat area of the pavement after soaking it with water the previous evening.

The day passed by peacefully until, in early evening, somebody in the back yard yelled out, "fire!" When I looked out the window, I saw smoke rising above the roof line of a building directly east of ours. My father and I ran downstairs and saw a number of men with buckets in their hands forming a long line to one of the adjoining buildings. My father became fully engaged in this rescue effort. I could not see the fire from where I was standing, but all seemed to be going well for a few minutes.

Then, German soldiers poised in the street decided to break up the rescue effort. Shots rang out. It was getting quite dark, but the square across which the men had to transport the water was in full view from the street. Since it would have been futile to continue, all of the men withdrew. No one was shot. Someone must have extinguished the blaze because the fire did not spread to our house during the night.

It was quiet the next morning, an ominous, eerie silence. In this lull, I began to speculate how long our 500 eggs would last before they went bad. There was no refrigeration in those days. It turned out that this was not a relevant concern because we had only one more meal in our apartment.

After lunch I smelled smoke, looked out the window and saw that the roof of the adjoining building, was on fire and the cinders were falling on our roof. It was only a matter of time before we would have to leave our apartment.

There was no time to pack anything. The smoke started to choke us. We started calling each other in a panic to get to the kitchen area and exit the apartment through the back staircase to the yard. The smoke and smell were becoming unbearable.

I decided to save my most valued possessions, namely my animals, a dog and a cat, and also the beautiful accordion my father bought me for my birthday the previous March. I grabbed my dog, which happened to be standing next to me, shoved him under my jacket (if he was a German shepherd this would not have worked) and wondered where my cat might be hiding. Under the stress of the moment I recalled that my Siamese long haired cat, called Kizia, was always very difficult to catch and hold; furthermore, she was extremely afraid of leaving our apartment.

God, did I hate that cat! One day, a few weeks earlier, I had managed to catch her and take her out to the back yard. As soon as I let her go, she ran right back to the house and up the stairs to our apartment. She then licked herself for hours to get rid of the smell of my hands from her beautiful hair. I decided to abandon her inside the smoke-filled apartment.

I found my accordion, grasped the handle of the carrying case in my right hand, while supporting the dog with my left, and ran outdoors for a whiff of fresh air. My parents were directly behind me.

We were not the only people outside in the back yard. There were about a hundred others whose lives were threatened in a similar way. Everybody seized what they could. Some took pillows and goose down bed covers with them, while others carried suitcases. I was happy with what I had, although I felt bad about abandoning Kizia.

Now what? What will happen next? These were questions that probably everyone was asking themselves. I do not recall hearing any conversations among the people gathered in front of their houses, just silence. After a few minutes of such transfixion, I heard loud and persistent banging, by what seemed like several people, on the cast iron gates separating us from the street. Soon after, a formation of German soldiers, with drawn bayonets, appeared out of the concrete arch hiding the gate and started to run in our direction.

I remember spontaneously raising my hands in prayer asking, "O God, could this be the end of my life? I haven't even started to live. I'm only 15 years old." When I finished saying this, the first soldier was already close to me and yelled out in German: "Follow us!" I whispered thanks to God. We were not going to be executed, just yet. With that the platoon leader turned around, while the other soldiers surrounded us, and we headed back to the street.

Across the street was the hotel Bristol, one of the premier hotels in Warsaw, our first destination. It never occurred to me to turn around and look at my house for the last time. I guess thoughts of survival were more important at that moment.

It was hard for me to carry that big and heavy accordion. I could not imagine myself able to carry it for any long distance. Soon we entered the hotel and were led into a large room in the basement. I don't have any recollection of the details of our stay there; which lasted two or three days.

In the middle of the night we were told to leave. With a heavy heart, I decided to leave my accordion behind in the basement of the hotel. My parents agreed.

It was spooky and dark when we left under heavy guard. There were no streetlights; no moon. I was unable to see my house. By then, the fire must have consumed it and the cinders had cooled down. It was pitch dark. My thoughts went out to Kizia. I hoped that she perished from asphyxiation rather than being burned by the fire.

It was fortunate that the weather was reasonably warm in the middle of summer that year. There had been no time to look for clothes before we had to evacuate the building. I was wearing house slippers instead of regular street shoes and I soon became painfully aware of how inappropriate this was.

After crossing a large square called Plac Piłsudskiego we entered Ogród Saski (Saski Garden). This time, there were German troops everywhere. Some of the soldiers had facial features that I had never seen before—large faces with pronounced cheekbones and relatively small noses. As I found out later, these were Mongolians from inside Russia who were fighting alongside the Germans in order to gain independence for their province from their Soviet masters. They frightened me.

We stood in a long column, several persons wide. There were many more people there than just those from our apartment complex. We heard rumors that older individuals would be separated and executed because they could be of no use to the German Fatherland. Also, there were fears that young women might be raped. However, to my knowledge, nothing like this happened while I was there. After we spent an hour or so in the garden, we were told to start walking again.

Soon after we left the garden and the trees were not blocking the view, I saw a panorama of fire. As far as I could see in any direction, all of the buildings were ablaze. This time, unlike the year before when I rode my bike on the outside of the wall of a burning ghetto, I found myself in the middle of a conflagration. Down the street that we had to walk, houses on both sides were on fire. The trick was to avoid flying debris, which was often red hot. Bricks were strewn all over, some of them hot to the touch. I wasn't getting much protection for my feet by walking in house slippers!

This part of town that we were crossing must have seen ferocious fighting between the German troops and the inhabitants of the city. I kicked something soft while trying to avoid a flying cinder. When I looked down, it was the body of a man.

People were walking much lighter now, most of their belongings having been dropped along the way. Everything imaginable was abandoned on the sides of the safest path that the people before me charted as they proceeded down the street.

By morning we arrived in Pruszków, a suburb of Warsaw. My dog appeared to be quite happy.

Mathew's Father, Bolesľaw Sikorski

The Rescue

Pruszków was a town of about 10,000 inhabitants. It was comforting to see a quaint little city asleep. There were no houses on fire. All appeared to be peaceful here. I was annoyed, though, that no one seemed to notice us. We were a mass of refugees who left their belongings in a burning city.

One thing appeared strange to me in our continued march through Pruszków. After we crossed two or three sets of railroad tracks, the street veered off to the right. In the fog of dawn, I was able to recognize a fence directly ahead of us. There were many massive, hangar-like buildings behind the fence.

At first I had no idea where we were headed, but soon my curiosity was satisfied. As we got closer, it became clear that the long line of humanity ahead of us was fading behind a large gate separating us from the fenced-in area. As I got closer to the gate, I could read a large sign located over a very wide wrought iron entry gate. The sign said "Zakłady Kolejowe," ("Railroad Works".) Slowly, the reality of the situation began to dawn on me. We were headed for trains. The most frightening thought I had was, "Is our destination going to be Germany and forced labor, or worse, incarceration in a Nazi concentration, or extermination camp?"

These thoughts filled my heart with utmost concern. I had read numerous reports in the underground press about the Nazi concentration camps before the start of the Warsaw Uprising. This type of reading had to be done with the greatest of care, so that no one could possibly see us doing this. If someone happened to observe illicit bulletins in our hands, and reported us to the police, the punishment was incarceration and death.

The procedure we followed was to go to one of the rooms in our apartment that faced the street. If we read on the floor, using special lights that could be pulled almost completely down to the floor, no one would be able to see us from the street. The buildings across from our apartment were relatively far away and did not house any people. One was a church and the other two were government buildings in the hands of German military authorities.

I wondered, "What will become of my family? Will I be able to remain with my parents, or are we going to be separated? What will happen to my dog Enia?"

Once we were inside the fence, I noticed that the railroad tracks were all ending in those large, hangar-like structures that I had noticed earlier. I found out later that these buildings were constructed before the war to house railroad cars and locomotives for painting and other necessary repairs. During the war, however, they were used by the German occupiers to hold large numbers of people - two to three thousand per building. It was a holding station prior to shipment by train to Germany or wherever the concentration camps were located. These buildings provided shelter at night and easy access to trains during the day.

In mid-afternoon of the same day, my parents and I found ourselves in one of the far corners of one of those buildings. There was nothing inside except a multitude of people: men, women, and children, haggard looking and very tired after an all-night walk. We did not recognize anybody there from our neighborhood. There really wasn't much to talk about, but it was wonderful that at least we had one another.

About a half an hour after our arrival and after everyone found a place to stand or sit, a voice came from huge loudspeakers saying, "All adult males are to evacuate the building immediately, women and children are to remain inside." There were no exceptions and we knew it.

It took some time for the men to leave considering the tears and emotional good-byes of uttering perhaps the last words ever to each other. Time was also necessary for men to simply push themselves through the crowd to the exit door, which happened to be located in front of the building.

After all the men had left, it became relatively quiet

inside, except for sporadic sobbing. My mother was not crying, neither was I. However, I do vividly recall having been overcome by a feeling of great uneasiness inside after my father's departure. This feeling was followed by a thought, "If I don't do something right away, I will never see my father again!" In spite of an awesome fear, which felt like a vice squeezing me on all sides, I decided that this horrible situation perpetrated against us required immediate and resolute action on my part.

I was unable to think of exactly what I could and should do, but decided to take one action at a time. Possible consequences of my actions did not even enter my mind. I was totally convinced that time was of the essence in this situation. First I turned to my mother, handed Enia to her, and said, "Mother, I want to rescue my father. I don't have any idea where he is, but I do want to bring him back here, so that we can be together again." She did not reply, not just yet. I can still recall that special solemn look on her face!

Two women who were standing nearby, close enough to have overheard what I had said to mother, angrily tried to convince her that she should not let me out of her sight. One of the women said, "Are you crazy? As soon as he takes a step outside of this building he will be shot." As if in reply to this warning, my mother turned back to me and said, "Maciej, if you feel in the depth of you heart that you will succeed, go ahead and do it."

Her approval was the only thing I needed! I immediately turned around and started to push myself through the crowd toward the door through which the men were led out of the building.

Once I reached the door and opened it, I was confronted with the following scenario. There were three buildings on my right, similar to the one I was about to leave, between a freight train and me. The boxcars appeared to be filled to capacity with men. My father had to be somewhere on that train!

I had to make a decision. It seemed foolish to start running toward the train because there were five German soldiers between the train and me. They were standing, equally spaced, and fully armed with sub-machine guns. These soldiers were strategically located in the middle of the street that led to the train, between each set of buildings on both sides of the street. They were there to see to it that order was preserved and no one would leave from any of the buildings.

The soldier closest to me was standing about half way between the building I was about to exit and the building on the other side of the street. The train full of men was to my right. Not wanting to risk being shot for disturbing the order that the soldiers were assigned to keep, I ran to the soldier closest to me. He was only a few feet away.

When I got there, he appeared to be quite surprised. The good thing was that he wasn't about to shoot me. Although a beginner with the German language, I was able to communicate that, "My mother is in this building and my father is somewhere on the train; can you help me get him back so my family can be reunited?"

He replied with obvious respect, "I am sorry, I cannot help you because I am not allowed to move from where I am standing. Go and talk to the soldier who is closer the train." And so I did. All of the other soldiers said approximately the same thing as I was getting closer to the train. The men on the train appeared to be agitated; I had attracted their attention.

Finally the soldier closest to the train said, "If you look to the right, in the direction of the locomotive, you will be able to see the officer of this operation. Talk to him, he might be able to help you." With these reassuring words I turned around and immediately spotted the man that he was talking about.

He was obviously a soldier of high rank with all sorts of decorations on his uniform, a very tall and imposing figure like in the stories of Teutonic Knights I used to read. He was not alone. There were two adjutants, one on each side of him. They were all slowly walking toward me. Once I was sure who I needed to talk to, I ran as fast as I could alongside the train in order to talk to the officer.

As soon as they noticed me, the soldiers stopped, probably wondering what this kid wanted.

Upon arrival, I stood in front of the big man in the middle and told him, essentially, what I had communicated to the other soldiers. After a short pause he said, "But, where is your father?" I answered, "I don't know, exactly; he is somewhere on this train." He replied, "Okay, let's walk beside the train until we find him."

Pandemonium broke out among the men on the train. Apparently, they could not grasp the meaning of what they saw, a teenage boy walking with German soldiers as if taking a stroll on a Sunday afternoon.

We passed a few cars with some men watching us and others shouting until I heard my father yell out in Polish from one of the cars ahead of us, "Maciej, what are you doing here? Go back to mother or they will shoot you!"

I replied, also in Polish, while making a big assumption as if it were already a reality, "Come down. You are allowed to get off the train and join mother and me." After some apparent commotion inside the car, my father was pushed out by a man behind him and fell to the ground. By the time my soldier friends and I had arrived, my father had just finished dusting off his trousers. He did not appear to have suffered any injury during the fall.

Once we were close, the head German officer asked me if this was my father. After I said yes, to my big surprise - he stretched out his hand to my father in a friendly gesture and said, "I am pleased to meet you and mentioned his name. My father reciprocated and they shook hands. Then the German said to me, "Now, you show me where your mother is, I also would like to meet her." I was ecstatic!

"Where is she?" He inquired. I pointed to the building where I left her and the German said, "Let's go and join her." As we proceeded, the five soldiers along the way who were entrusted with keeping order saluted the officer with the typical clicking of the heels of their boots. I suddenly felt very important and proud of myself.

As soon as I opened the door to the building where my mother was located, my father and I walked in first with the soldiers behind us. When the women and children closest to the door saw the five of us, they began to make room in the direction that I indicated. As soon as we arrived, the officer asked me, "Is this your mother?" I said, "Yes," and he stretched out his hand to her in greeting. Then he said, "I am very pleased to meet you Madam" and turning to me he asked a question that I never would have expected, "Now that you are together as a family, is there anything else I can do for you?"

I was completely dumbfounded. I looked for words to express my appreciation to him for what he had already done for us. I was the only youngster in this crowd who had his father with him! In my joy I could not think of anything else he could do. And so, I stretched out my hand to him and thanked him for fulfilling my wish of being reunited with my father. With that the German soldiers turned and left.

To this day, I wonder what prompted this man to show compassion to one fifteen- year-old boy while sending untold thousands of people to Nazi concentration camps every day. The Polish Jews from the Warsaw ghetto were taken first and then non-Jewish Poles from other parts of the city of Warsaw. Was he a good man doing his job in Hell?

The last good-bye

After an afternoon heaving with emotions, we spent the night peacefully, rejoicing in each other's company. We did not get much physical rest, because there were no beds, only some straw on the concrete floor. We awakened early the next morning. Soon after dawn a call came over the loudspeakers to get ready to evacuate the building. Nothing was said of where we were to go, but it was clear to me that the immediate destination had to be the train. Thank God, whatever the destination, we were optimistic that this time we would be able to stay together.

As soon as we left the building we had to make an effort not to lose each other because of the crowds of people milling around. Once again, I became aware of how fortunate we were that my mission to rescue my father had succeeded the previous day. The people we saw this morning were mostly walking in family groups. The directive for separation of families the day before must not have been issued in other buildings. This time, all the people were told to leave.

A train stood in the same place as the one from which I rescued my father the day before. This time it was empty - waiting for us. As if prodded by an invisible guide, the crowd moved slowly in the direction of the train.

As we slowly progressed toward the train, my mother suddenly recognized a good friend of hers from childhood days who wore a Red Cross armband on her left arm. She prodded my father and me to change direction in order to catch up with her friend. Her name was Lucy. She was in a great hurry and walked against the crowd. She recognized my mother instantly and they warmly embraced and kissed.

Lucy told us that the reason why she was wearing the armband was because she was employed as a nurse at a field hospital located at the rail yard property in the vicinity of the train station. This was the location from which the officer was coming when I first engaged him with my plea to free my father from the train.

After Lucy said that she was free to leave the compound for the night and come back to work the next day, I remember my mother asking her, "Lucy, since we do not know what will happen to us after getting on this train, I wonder if you could take this can?" My mother pulled out an aluminum can from her large handbag and asked, "Will you deliver it whenever you can to my good friend, Maria, in Bielanów (a Warsaw suburb)?" Lucy said that she would be glad to do it.

This can, which at one time must have contained coffee and now, to my surprise, was used by mother as a treasure chest, had in it some cash, gold coins, two of my mother's diamond rings and my father's silver cigarette case. This cigarette case was gold-plated inside. He received it from the participants of a course that he taught in 1937. He cherished this memento greatly because all the names of his listeners were engraved on the gold-plated area inside. These were the only material possessions that we had. With Lucy's acceptance, my mother and father no longer had to worry about this family treasure being lost or being stolen. Of course, I still had my most valued possession, my dog, Enia.

Lucy told us that her function in the field hospital was to help people who got sick and to act as an interpreter from Polish to German for the doctor, who was German. Often, she said, patients who were very sick were permitted to leave the compound to freedom. I remember my feelings of envy toward Lucy, jealous of her freedom to come and go from the rail yard as she pleased. I never had a chance to find out how she was able to be in such an enviable position in those

A few minutes after her departure, I was stunned! Among the crowd was the officer, the man who allowed my father to join us in the assembly building the day before. I yelled out to my parents, "Stay here!" and ran to talk to the officer. This time he was by himself, no adjutants. He was dressed very differently from the day before, no fancy uniform and no decorations on his chest. He also appeared to be in a great hurry and, like Lucy, moved in a direction opposite to that of the crowd.

I intercepted him. He stopped and looked down at me in a friendly manner. Right then I knew that he recognized me from the day before. I asked him point blank, "Can you get us out of here? Yesterday you asked me whether there was anything else you could do for us." To that he replied, "I am sorry, but today I cannot help you. Good luck." With that he resumed his gait. I thought "Why did I not think of asking him for freedom the day before?"

I rejoined my parents and we resumed walking slowly toward the train. Soon we stood in front of the entrance to a boxcar. We were the first ones in line to get in. This was not a sleeper, not even a passenger car. There were no seats inside. The interior was swept clean and was completely empty.

We climbed aboard helping each other negotiate two high steps from the ground to the floor of the car. I stood in the back of the car, under a small opening in the wall located just under the ceiling. The opening was about one foot high and two feet wide. It was crisscrossed with barbed wire so no one would attempt to escape from the car.

My parents were standing right beside me. My mother suggested that I sit down on the floor, which I did. However, I realized that to remain sitting might be soon difficult because there were more and more people climbing into our car. Enia was sitting in my lap. He appeared to be getting quite fidgety with all of these strangers crowding around. Chihuahuas tend to be independent thinkers. He stayed quiet though, which assured his not being taken away from me. About 80 people (and one small dog) must have been packed into our train car.

This is all that I remember about the trip to Germany, which lasted several days. I don't have any recollection of how we slept, ate, and went to the bathroom. All of my memories of the rest of the trip have been erased. I only remember the morning, at the end of that journey, when we arrived in the vicinity of a concentration camp north of Berlin. My father lifted me up to the opening and I saw in big black letters on a white background the ominous words "Sachsenhausen-Oranienburg." I remembered this name from the underground press, which we used to read at home in Warsaw. The name of this town was synonymous with a slave-labor camp from which people were not returning home. I sensed that we were in for some hard times.

Once we reached the railroad station, the order came for everyone to leave the train. Traveling on foot, the group snaked across the beautiful little town of Oranienburg about 3,000 strong, including men, women and children. Both sides of the streets were lined with single-family houses, very clean with red roofs and little gardens full of vegetables and flowers. In front, little children were playing and occasionally a youngster would yell out "Polnische Banditen" (Polish bandits). We knew then that we were arriving not as guests, but as slaves.

The greatest fear mounted in my heart when a column of some one-hundred men in striped prison clothes, guarded by well-armed German soldiers and accompanied by salivating German shepherd dogs, appeared from the opposite direction. Is this what awaits my father and me? None of the prisoners passing by dared to lift their head for even a brief moment to look at us. Soon they were gone. Only a cloud of dust remained in the air for a while.

After a long walk we came to a large square surrounded by military barracks. When everybody from the train had arrived at this location, a message came over the loudspeakers. "You have had a long journey and you need a shower. Everybody line up in four columns: men alone, males 14 years of age and up, women alone and women with small children." There was a lot of consternation. What would this mean? Once separated, would we be able to find each other again? My parents and I huddled together to decide what to do. The dog will stay with mother, and father and I will walk to our respective columns. I was 15

Mathew's Mother, Jadwiga Sikorski in 1941

years old then; therefore, I should not be standing with either of my parents.

Once in my column, I stood in the outside line facing an open square. My father was to the right of me in the men's column. I could see him clearly from where I was standing.

Suddenly, I saw a German soldier slowly walking across the square in the direction of the boy's column. He stopped right in front of me. The first thing I noticed was that he wore glasses, but that was not all, he could see through his right eye only. His left eyeball was invisible and appeared to be covered with a strip of skin. This was not a pleasant sight! I was confused for a moment, but soon he started talking in perfect Polish, "Boys, listen to me, look at my eye," pointing to his invisible left eye. "I was living in Poland on the German border when the war started. When that part of Poland was incorporated into the German Reich, I was conscripted to serve in the German Army. Because I initially refused, I was tortured. This is why I lost sight in my left eye." His statement filled me with such a deep awareness of the gravity of the situation, that I felt inclined to follow any of his future suggestions. He spoke with such a soft voice that only the boys closest to me could have possibly heard the message that followed.

He continued, "If you have your mother with you,

join her immediately and go with her to the column of women with children. However, if you don't have your mother here, pick someone from the column of single women to be your surrogate mother and beg her to go with you to the column of women with children." With that he slowly turned around and walked away. That is how my mother and I were saved from going to the concentration camp and were able to survive the war.

After the soldier's departure I ran to my mother and told her the message that some of the fortunate boys were able to hear. She decided that we would follow his instructions right after we said good-bye to my father. We found my father easily and shared with him what we intended to do. This was a very solemn moment for me, which I will never forget as long as I live. We hugged and we kissed performing a juggling act with Enia. We passed him from my hands to my mother's and vice-versa. Finally, my father, looking directly into mother's eyes said, "Dziudziuś," (this was his most endearing way of addressing her) "Could it be that I have already accomplished everything in my life?" She had no answer for him. His intuition was correct, again!

First, men alone, then boys and finally women alone were led away to, "take a shower." My mother and I spent the night under the stars with the other women and children wondering what the future might bring. The following morning we were loaded on the next available train.

Journey to Hameln

After being separated from my father, I followed the suggestion of the German soldier with one eye to go with my mother to the group of women with children. Mother told me, "Sit down here," which was in the center of the group. I was fairly tall for my age, and she figured I could escape possible detection of being in the "wrong" group better by being seated. This measure, in retrospect, wasn't really necessary because no one, I'm sure, carried any personal documentation with which anyone's age could be checked. Everybody was forcibly taken out of Poland so there was no need for birth certificates or passports.

My family was now reduced to three: my mother, Enia and me. As soon as we sat down, Enia jumped into my hands. Soon after, an order was given over huge loudspeakers located around the square, "The column of adult men is to leave the square and follow the guards." There was no more talk about taking a shower after a long trip! Next came the order for the young men to leave. The young men were those who either hadn't heard the mystery soldier's message, or perhaps, had decided to disregard it thinking that it would be okay to just remain where they were and that nothing bad was going to happen to them. Finally, the order came for single women to leave. It was getting dark by then and the only people allowed to stay in the square were the women with children. It looked like we were going to spend the night in the open air.

I was overwhelmed with grief. I was deeply aware of the fact that the peace and stability of my life up to this point could never be the same without my father. I kept recalling what a wonderful life I'd had prior to the Warsaw Uprising. My thoughts went back to the day Janek, one of my dearest friends who often came to my house to play and for feasts of fried potatoes, admiringly said, "Maciej, you have all the toys." I happened to be sitting, at that moment, on my bicycle and my dog, Enia, was happily stuck under my coat with his head protruding from it. Janek's head was too close to Enia's. He suddenly got his hair ruffled severely by the furiously growling and barking dog. How dare he talk to his master that way!

As I recalled several similar happy memories from Warsaw, I kept coming back to the reality of my present situation. I was very grateful for being saved along with my mother from being taken to the concentration camp by the wonderful man in the German uniform who undoubtedly risked his life to prevent our permanent separation.

I started asking painful questions: "How long will we be separated from my father? When will the war end? Will my father be able to survive the stay in the concentration camp?" I fully realized that the prognosis was not good, based on what I knew about Nazi camps from the "underground" press in Warsaw.

My mother tried to console me the best she knew how. In her heart, though, she must have been hurting deeply, as well. Our future looked bleak indeed. We did not have any knowledge about what we might be told to do and where we would be taken from Sachsenhausen, in the vicinity of Berlin.

We spent the night under a clear, cloudless sky. There was no moon, but the sight of brilliant stars arranged in a multitude of constellations in the Milky Way was absolutely breathtaking. There was a chill in the air, which is normally not unusual for the end of August in Northern Europe; but I do not recall being cold. My mother and I were huddled together and our dog was, of course, with us. The air was completely still. If there were any wind in this completely open, very large square, we would have been quite cold. My Enia was comfortably stuck under my jacket and we were warming each other. It must have been rather uncomfortable, to say the least, to spend the night in this way without any pillows or blankets, just sitting on the concrete surface of the square.

The following morning all women with children who were in the square were told to walk to the railroad station to be loaded onto a boxcar. There must have been a few hundred of us. Perhaps this was the same train that brought us to Germany from Poland the day before. I missed my father very much! I do not recall having been given anything to eat or drink during this painful stop in Sachsenhausen-Oranienburg, although it did not seem to matter. The events themselves were all-consuming. I am surprised that the dog appeared to be happy. I guess all he needed was to be with us!

We were not informed about where we were going; it didn't seem to matter, because there was nothing we could do about it. I did not engage in fearful thinking about the future. I was brimming with gratitude to God for having been able to spend a few more days with my father and for sparing my mother and me from separation, at least for the time being.

The Polish-speaking German soldier had helped me avoid being confined to the Nazi concentration camp, which I am sure I could not have survived. I knew I had a defective heart since birth. Had it not been for my wonderful parents who truly loved me very much and did everything possible in Warsaw to keep me as healthy as medical science allowed in those days, I would not have survived to reach fifteen years of age. Considering the inhumane living conditions in the Nazi concentration camps, I would not have lasted long before acquiring bronchitis or pneumonia, which without proper care would have quickly put an end to my life.

I don't recall how long our journey was from the vicinity of Berlin to the Bergen-Belsen concentration camp. The camp is located about half way between Berlin and Hanover. Again, I do not have any memory of this trip! From the railroad station we were told to march to an area of the camp where there were a lot of people. Most of them were there already when we arrived. I observed that they were sitting, reclining or sleeping on the floor, which was covered with straw. The building was very large, similar to the one near Warsaw where we had spent the night. It consisted of a semicircular roof and walls. Because the other two sides were completely open, it was possible to hide under the roof without opening any doors. There were no fences in sight.

I thought that it would be nice to eat something. I do not recall having been given anything to eat since we left the basement of the Bristol Hotel in Warsaw. Thinking about food, I suddenly felt the need to go to the bathroom. Since I did not know where it was located, I asked a soldier standing close to me. He told me that I needed to go to the other side of the structure where a large number of people were resting. I carefully threaded my way through the crowd to the other side and nearly fainted upon seeing the so-called "bathroom." It was a huge outdoor pit, about 100 yards square. It was filled with reeking excrement and was spanned from one side to the other with a wooden bridge about three feet wide. The bridge structure was supported by a series of wooden poles driven into the bottom of the pit. If I could, I would have walked away in disgust. However, all the forces of nature were telling me to proceed. When I stepped on the wooden planks, I was quickly convinced that this was not a very stable structure. I had to walk very carefully in order not to drown in the muck below. I intended to go as far as I could, away from thousands of people surrounding the pit. I really did not want to expose myself to anybody. All sorts of thoughts were running through my mind. "Were the soldiers who built this pit the 'Kultur Traeger,' those who were supposedly bringing culture to the 'uncivilized' people of Europe? How was it possible to conceive and build such a monstrosity without any regard whatsoever for human feelings? Where was the consideration for natural, wholesome self-consciousness that can be expected in normal people?" After a while, I concerned myself only with my personal safety, in order to be able to return to mother and Enia.

A short time after the "bathroom" ordeal, my little dog Enia found himself in danger. A handsome, young German soldier came close to me and said, "I do not know where you and your mother will go from here, and whether you will be able to keep your dog; therefore, I want you to let me have your dog! I have a wife and two young children who would take good care of this dog." To this I replied, "I came here from Warsaw, my house was burned down and I lost all my toys, my father was taken away from us in Sachsenhausen; therefore, I cannot and I will not give you my dog, because he is all I have!" Subsequently, the soldier walked away empty-handed. I felt so grateful to my parents for seeing to it that I had learned enough German to be able to defend my interests under dire circumstances.

Glory, glory, hallelujah! Finally, some food arrived in big metal kettles. Everybody received a funny-looking cup, which resembled a military helmet, except smaller, held upside down. (These cups are on display in the Jewish Holocaust Museum in Washington, D.C.) It felt good to have something to eat! People lined up as someone holding a large ladle partially filled our "cups." What we received was a thick, cooked mixture of different vegetables. It tasted good, but I wished that someone had taken greater care in peeling the potatoes and made sure that the vegetables were well washed prior to cooking. Then sand would not have been one of the ingredients. The most important thing for me was that my Enia liked the meal and I was still his owner!

Innocence and Reality

We spent the night outdoors, lying on top of picnic tables that were standing in front of the already overcrowded building. The next morning we found ourselves back on the train, not knowing our destination.

Three feet from death

After my father was taken to the Nazi Sachsenhausen-Oranienburg concentration camp, my mother and I traveled across Germany in a box car with all the other women and children until we reached the picturesque little town of Hameln. Hameln is located about 30 miles south of Hanover, Germany.

After arrival, 80 women and their children were told to leave the train. My mother and I were in this group. We were led under the guard of heavily armed German soldiers to the outskirts of the city where several factories were located. This must have been the industrial and rail transport hub for this area of Germany. In the suburb, the streets were crisscrossed with railroad tracks all leading to a textile plant, an aircraft factory and a heavy machinery plant.

I had never seen such huge metal parts as those being manufactured there. The doors in the large, hangar-like building were swung wide open, as we were walking by, so I could easily see what was inside. I became quite curious about what they were for, but it was impossible to ask anybody. We were being led as prisoners and had to follow the guards without the opportunity to step aside and ask questions. Perhaps these were turbine drives for submarines. The structure, about thirty feet long and six feet in diameter, was a series of cylinders joined together by a single shaft. After a good walk we finally arrived at our destination, which was a factory building with a very high ceiling consisting of glass panes to provide light during the day. The building was completely empty inside except for an appropriate number of double-decker bunk beds sufficient to house all the women with their children. As it turned out, we were all supposed to work in the adjoining factories. After a while we adjusted to our living conditions and tried to make the best of them. Our situation was such that there was no place to escape, even if anyone had wanted to. Under these circumstances, our German bosses thought there was no need to have any guards around us.

Personally, I felt relatively free in my endeavors; nobody stopped me from collecting frozen potatoes after work. A lot of potatoes were still buried in the ground after the harvest in the adjoining fields on one side of our "home." When I gave them to my mother she would cook a delicious potato soup (I always loved potato soup). The soup tasted even better after we received a large package of lard from my uncle who had a farm in Poland and stayed there during the Warsaw Uprising, thus avoiding being taken to Germany against his will. The lard supplied the necessary fat for our diet, which really consisted only of potatoes, bread (which could be purchased with rationing cards that we received from the factory) and fish salad, which I could buy without restrictions, from a store in town. I could also buy a few grams of ham every so often, but only when I held my dog under my arm. The ham was only allowable for my dog. Since he often was unwilling to chew the ham by himself, I usually would chew it for him. This procedure provided me with the taste of ham. Not only that, since Enia ate so little, my mother and I could have some ham too, in the soup.

Going out to collect potatoes in the late afternoon also afforded to me the opportunity to excitedly listen to the rhythmic drone of hundreds and hundreds of fully loaded Allied bombers flying toward Hannover, Berlin and other major German cities. Although I felt bad about the fact that terror and loss of life would ensue for the inhabitants of German cities, I felt that this action was necessary to help end the war quickly and bring my father back.

We continued to live in this building until the end of World War II. Enia did not seem to be particularly perturbed about living in such unusual quarters. He slept with me on the upper berth, while my mother occupied the bed below. I am surprised that in all this time (several months) the dog never once fell off the upper berth. I must have been a skillful dog keeper and psychologist, rapidly responding to his natural needs.

The factory in which my mother and I were

employed manufactured blankets for the German military. My mother was taught how to operate a loom, a new profession for her since she was trained in Poland to be an elementary school teacher. I was initially employed in the same factory as an errand boy, most of the time watching for empty bobbins on spinning frames and exchanging them for full ones. Later on, after a severe illness during which I nearly died, my life was saved by a Yugoslav doctor who stole hard-to-get injection medication from a German supply store and administered it to me while I was in a coma. Afterward I was given a very easy job in an aircraft factory next door. My job consisted of neatly arranging freshly manufactured small metal parts in large trays for storage. It was a sit-down job, enabling me to recover quickly from my illness.

One beautiful day in the spring of 1945, I decided to leave my dog with my mother in the building during lunch break and go play by myself in the nearby creek, tributary to the Weser River. The creek was located near the factory building where we lived. When I got to the creek, which was about 75 feet wide, I took my shoes off and waded into the water. I wore shorts that day and the water was only about one to two feet deep, so it was easy to move around without getting my clothes wet.

Next to fishing, my favorite water activity was

skipping stones. I looked for smooth ones which when thrown at an appropriate angle would repeatedly skip on the surface of the water. I spent a few minutes doing this and enjoying myself thoroughly. Suddenly, I heard the roar of aircraft engines. The sound, which was getting louder and louder, came from behind a mountain located in the back of the factory buildings. Very soon I saw an unusual looking twin-boomed, twin-engine American plane climb steeply from behind the mountain on my left, which was a few miles away, make a loop high up in the distance and slowly turn toward the river in which I was wading. As it started to align itself with the river and head in my direction, I noticed a second and a third plane following a similar flight path, and then the fourth and fifth.

At the moment when the first plane started to come down from a high altitude loop, I sensed what was about to happen. Between the airplane and me stood a freight train, which happened to have stopped with its locomotive being located in the middle of the bridge that spanned the river. I knew then that the airplanes must have been going after the locomotive! Following this sudden realization came a silent, inner, extrasensory command, "Hide under a bush." My Guardian Angel must have been standing by! I instinctively turned ninety degrees to the right. I was much closer to the right shore of the river and saw a bush. The bush was about five feet high and a few feet away from the edge of the water. I darted out of the water, ran for the bush and hid among the lowest branches trying to make myself invisible.

Almost immediately after my escape from the water, I heard the first airplane release a volley of bullets from a machine gun toward the locomotive. The machine gun was located in the center section of the airplane right in front of the pilot. As the airplane started to level its flight path over the water, bullets impacted the water with a loud splashing sound. Some bullets managed to break up a number of stones on the bottom of the river sending a shower of debris in all directions. Two stone fragments nearly hit me as they landed very close to the bush where I was hiding.

As the first plane was passing me by, flying only a few feet above water, I was deeply impressed by the size of the machine gun that now was silent, and the total concentration on the part of the pilot who was now attempting to make his quick getaway. He proceeded to rev up the engines of his plane to climb quickly in order to escape powerful anti-aircraft fire coming from several ground-based machine guns manned by German soldiers in the vicinity of the factory buildings.

Before I had a chance to mentally wish the first pilot farewell, the second airplane arrived. This plane scored a hit. What a show! The high caliber bullets punctured the locomotive's high pressure chamber releasing clouds of steam grotesquely rising towards the heavens with a loud hiss, trying to tell the story of the might of the Third Reich that was going up in smoke. After the second airplane came a third, fourth and fifth. The job was well done. The succeeding planes pumped more bullets into the locomotive to make sure that the train had been stopped for good. With each passing plane I kept hearing more and more splashing sounds of bullets hitting the water close to me, but miraculously, I was unharmed.

The incredible "show" was soon over. When it ended I was trembling all over. I got up and my legs felt like jelly. In a few minutes, though, I was able to run to mother and Enia, praying all the way, to tell them what had happened. My mother did not ask any questions, but held me in her arms until I stopped shaking. My Enia ran to me and all was well again!

A day or two later rumors reached me that the ground-based machine guns managed to down one of the attacking Lockheed P-38 Lightning attack fighters. I also heard that the pilot of the downed plane did not perish and was taken prisoner.

On that memorable day, I happened to be a witness to one episode of the Allies' concerted action to systematically destroy German locomotives. The purpose of this was to paralyze rail traffic across Germany.

The Author dwarfed by a Lockheed P-38 Lightning attack plane like the one that almost shot him while aiming for the locomotive. It was on display at a recent local air show.

Hell was only 50 yards away

A few days after my scary encounter with the American P-38 attack planes, I walked out of the factory building after work hoping to enjoy the remainder of the beautiful day. The sky was cloudless; the air was crisp and clear. No radar confusing aluminum strips were glistening in the sun's rays, perhaps because it was late afternoon. During the day the sky was usually full of these strips everywhere I looked. The visibility on this day, however, was perfect. The birds were singing, communicating with each other before the night. The setting sun over the factory building was casting a gorgeous golden hue over the meadow, which extended off to my left in the direction of the river. I will never forget it.

In front of me, about fifty yards away, was the large factory building where the peculiar-looking large metal parts were being manufactured. I kept thinking and wondering, "Could this type of a factory be of use to me in the future to manufacture a vehicle that could fly, ride on water and also be used as a personal automobile?"

Back in Poland I made engineering plans to some day build such a vehicle, which I named, "stratomorziem." Translated into English the name stands for: strato-, stratosphere; mor-, ocean, or water; and ziem-, earth, or ground, a sort of a present day hovercraft, except very small, for only one or two occupants. I suddenly became distracted by the undulating drone of what sounded like a low-flying large aircraft coming from the east. I thought, "What kind of a plane could this be?"

Before I had a chance to intellectually go into different possibilities, I noticed, just clearing the top of a hill behind the sun-lit meadow, a huge military airplane, which looked like the bombers that I normally observed flying very high during the day. However, this plane was flying in the opposite direction, as if on a return path and oh, so very, very slowly. It almost looked like it was standing still in the air, or levitating. This was a magnificent sight. The setting sun illuminated the bottom of the airplane. It was dark olive green, almost black. The typical American markings on the wings were clearly visible. I thought: "This is my friend!" and I experienced a warm fuzzy, a glow around my heart, which slowly spread to the rest of my body. The plane seemed to be telling me, "Don't I look pretty?"

Next a pragmatic question came to my mind, "What is this plane doing here in the late afternoon, flying so low and why so very slowly?" If this is an American plane, and there wasn't any doubt about it, "Why hasn't the air raid alarm been sounded" and "Why are the anti-aircraft guns silent; where is everybody?"

When the plane was about twenty to thirty feet from the factory building, huge bay doors started to open in its belly. Initially, I only saw a lengthwise gap and after a short hesitation, the gap was getting wider and wider. What a sight!

Suddenly, it seemed as if somebody had inverted a garbage can over the opening in the plane and some strange longitudinal stick-like objects started to fall toward the factory roof. These sticks did not look like bombs, they did not have the well-known shape of a bomb; they were just tumbling end over end and in all directions. When the plane was exactly over the factory building, all hell broke loose! First, loud explosions and then fire, fire, and more fire - a sea of fire! Coupled with that was the scream of air raid sirens and furious anti-aircraft machine gun fire. The sticks turned out to be phosphorous incendiary bombs. Within minutes the entire factory building was in flames and inside, the big metal parts that I was so curious about, were burning.

I turned around in an instant and ran for my life to my mother who had not seen any of the action since she stayed inside our textile factory "home." I found out that she had only heard the explosions and sirens and was worried about me. Such was the destruction of one of three factories in our vicinity. Within hours there remained only a heap of rubble. Even the concrete sidewalks in front of the burned-out building were scorched.

Now that I am describing what happened more than sixty years ago, I realize that my childhood war games were replayed in actuality. What I'd created in my environment-bred innocence became real!

Children propagate what parents create. An acetone-filled syringe, a child's ingenious flamethrower, consumed paper buildings. Similarly, phosphorous-filled incendiaries devoured entire factories. A blackened area in the wooden floor of my parents' apartment was paralleled by scorched concrete sidewalks.

For me at the time, this was another step in the Allies' struggle to end the war. I felt so thankful that our textile factory was spared. If any of the bombs had landed only some sixty yards to the north, all of the women and children including myself would have been burned alive. I also give a lot of credit to the crew of the bomber for their courage to fly low enough to enable the bombardier to release his lethal cargo at exactly the right time to cause the total destruction of the intended target.

As for my feelings during this incident, I do not recall having any sensations of fear. At first, I thought, "What is going to happen next?" and when the puzzle resolved itself, I acted out my innate fight-or-flight response. I subconsciously accepted the reality of the situation and ran for cover.

In those days we were really living by one of the principles of what is now known as the Twelve Step program, "One day at a time." Our main concern was only to survive and to act the best we knew how. We truly lived in the present, because the past was history and the future—a mystery.

Not ready to die

The demolition of the adjoining factory had changed my mother's attitude toward air raid sirens. Before then she felt no compulsion to go to the air raid shelter when the sirens started to wail in spite of the fact that everyone else in the building did. I often felt insecure when she, Enia and I were the only ones remaining in the eighty plus person "dormitory," risking injury or loss of life. However, I was unable to muster enough courage to share my feelings with her and to join the others. The surprise bombing attack must have convinced her to take greater precautions in the future.

The next day, in the early afternoon, the alarm sounded. This time my mother said, "Maciej take Enia, we are going to the shelter." We got there while the sirens were still screaming. It wasn't far. All we had to do was to cross the lawn between our building and the main factory structure.

The shelter wasn't anything fancy. It consisted of a large room underneath the main factory building. In order to get inside, we walked through a large door opening and had to take three steps down to the floor. The entrance door was a thick steel plate and had such a large door handle that only a grown man or a strong woman could open or close it.

After all the women and children entered the shelter,

someone on the outside closed the door. For some reason there were no lights inside that room. It was very spooky. I snuggled up to my mother and held Enia between us. I prayed for a speedy end of the war and reunification with my father.

After a while the air raid sirens were turned off and there was total silence. We were all standing in the far corner of the shelter. Suddenly, I saw daylight, but only in the upper and lower corners of the door opening and merely for a second or so. A tremendous rush of air hit my face and the ground shook. Then, silence. I yelled out, "Mother, mother what was it?" But, to my surprise, I did not hear myself say anything. Neither did I hear her reply, if any. There was only dead silence. Then, I became aware of some vibration, some strange tingling sensation in my ears. In desperation I cried again, "Mama can you hear me? Why are you silent?" It was no use!

At this point my attention shifted to the sensations in my ears, the only signals from my body. Slowly, I calmed down and started to analyze what might have happened. I thought, "For that massive steel door to bend the way it did, the door lock must have been extremely strong. If it were not, the door would have swung wide open under the influence of such a powerful air blast. What caused this?" After a while, my hearing started to return. I was able to communicate with mother and also hear other people talk. I found out that my mother was also unable to hear for a while, just like the others.

I was elated that we could hear each other again, but the darkness in the room was truly oppressive. "When will the air raid end?"

My imagination soared to the future, to the time after the war when my family would be reunited again and we could buy a car. Before the war started, my parents were planning to buy a small car, a two seat Fiat, with extra space behind the front seats to accommodate my dog and me. I dreamed about this car every night and the rides we would take on weekends. I couldn't think of a greater joy for me in those days. The war changed all that.

My reverie was brutally interrupted and I was quickly brought back to reality when the sirens sounded announcing that the air raid was over. Almost immediately somebody from the outside slowly opened the door to the shelter so we could leave. It was wonderful to see daylight again. While holding my dog, I ran for the door. Since I was standing in the front row of people in the shelter, I managed to be the first person to get out. I could not believe what I saw. To my right lay a huge, unexploded bomb, as big as two beer barrels laid end-to-end, only one foot away from the factory wall and about two feet from the entrance door to the shelter. If it had detonated, the entire factory building would have been destroyed and we, in the shelter, would have vaporized. For me the moral of the story was, "Technology cannot be relied upon 100 percent." We were not ready to die!

I happily put my dog down on the ground so that he could obey nature. Enia became interested in the bomb and showed his respect the way male dogs do to a stationary object. The scene was hilarious since the bomb was probably a thousand times bigger than the dog. Pretty soon all of the people who came out of the shelter, as well as German factory officials and workers, gathered in disbelief around the bomb. It did not take long before everybody was chased away from the site to allow a team of demolition technicians to defuse and carry it away.

There was another surprise waiting for everybody as we returned to our factory "home." The majority of the glass panels in the ceiling had shattered, and pieces of glass were strewn all over the floor and beds. If my mother, Enia and I had remained inside the building during this air raid, we would have been seriously injured or perhaps even killed.

Liberation

After March 15th, 1945, the air raids in the Hameln area were so numerous that we could rarely put in a full day at work. Most of the time I would arrive on the job only to have to leave the building after a few minutes. The air raid sirens would start to wail and then, after a short while, be heard again to call the alarm off. This was the pattern of daily activities for nearly three weeks.

There were numerous American planes in the air. However, they were not in any kind of formation. They were crisscrossing the sky at will, occasionally dropping a small bomb here and there to halt or impede the rail traffic. These planes were not heavy bombers like the one that fire-bombed the factory next door. I was never a witness to any dogfights between the German and American planes. The skies were completely dominated by the U.S. Air Force.

In my gut, I felt that the end of the war was near. Life was so unstable with the constant wailing of sirens that work was impossible to complete. I thought, "This situation cannot last very long. Something has to happen. The question is what?" I did not observe any German troop movements, nor the building of fortifications. The city appeared to be completely defenseless should the Allies stage an attack.

As part of Hitler's "Forced Labor Force" we were not allowed to listen to the radio. This included not only programs from abroad, but also German broadcasts. If anyone was caught listening to the radio, he or she would be disposed of by the dreaded Gestapo. Thus, it was impossible for us to find out anything about the world situation. The German newspapers, (there were no others) continued to praise the progress of the "victorious German troops on all fronts." The expected German victory was imminent according to these enthusiastic reports in the papers. Yet the reality was different. The airspace did not appear to belong to the German Luftwaffe! Also, every night everyone could watch an awesome sight of clouds of fire descending on the city of Hanover, which was only about 30 miles away. I often wondered, "What else remains to be burned in that city? It should have been leveled a long time ago!"

On April 4th I went to work as usual. However, a big surprise awaited everyone upon arrival. The German Company officials and workers were nowhere in sight. They just disappeared! No communication or instructions of any kind were left for us by the Germans. We were left to our own resources. I felt somewhat uneasy about this sudden freedom. It did not take long for everyone in our building to get together to decide what to do next. Since the skies during the day were so full of American aircraft, we decided to quietly abandon the building and try to get to the outskirts of town. The city of Hameln is surrounded by wooded hills. This plan seemed logical in order to avoid being hit by a bomb or caught in cross-fire should fighting erupt between the approaching Allied armies and the German defenders.

We left the factory complex as quietly as we could and headed for the outskirts. It was not necessary to walk through the center of town in order to get away from inhabited areas. What surprised me after walking for a while was the total absence of German pedestrians as if a plague had hit the town. The city appeared to be completely deserted. No one watched us, tried to stop us, or interfered in any way with our plans to get away from the city. After all, we must have been clearly noticeable. We were a "parade" of 80 women with children mostly dressed in clothes made out of avocado-colored military blanket fabric. We also had a letter "P" (for Polish) sewn onto the outer garments located over our hearts to identify our national origin to the German population. Slowly, a feeling of assurance came over me that our escape would be successful. I felt wonderful.

After walking for an hour or so, we arrived at a road on the outskirts of town. On the opposite side of this road and over a small hill, was a forest. We had reached a safe place. Between the edge of the forest and the hill was a ravine that seemed just right for us to make camp and spend the night unseen and unheard by anyone. The hill provided protection from being noticed by whoever might be using the road.

I felt reassured that there might be no fighting in town when I saw two German soldiers running toward the forest only about 20 feet from us. They just glanced at us and proceeded with their escape. As they approached the woods both of them dropped their carbines on the ground and started to take off the tops of their uniforms while carrying civilian clothing in their hands. They were headed for home. For them the war was over. The question for me was, "What will happen next?"

Soon it was time to prepare for the night. Fortunately, it was fairly warm - the beginning of April. Everyone became situated on the ground as comfortably as possible with the bedding supplies that we had managed to bring with us. We were fortunate that it did not rain for a few days and the ground was dry. It was quite cozy. The hill was on one side of us, woods on the other and the tops of trees surrounded the ravine above. The sky was clear and full of stars. There was silence. I fell asleep right away.

I woke up at the crack of dawn the next morning. The date was April 5th, 1945. I was the first to awaken.

Everyone else was still asleep including my "watchful" dog. I opened my eyes and listened carefully. I thought I heard a noise coming from the road on the other side of the hill. The sound I was hearing was continuous and undulating as if coming from a heavy, slow moving vehicle. It did not resemble any sounds that I have ever heard before. It definitely could not be emanating from a moving automobile or a truck. It was a sort of a rumble, occasionally accompanied by a squeaking sound.

I asked myself, "Could that sound be coming from a tank?" And if so, "Was it a retreating German tank or a friendly American tank?" It certainly did not appear to be the sound of a fleeing vehicle; it was too quiet for that. I decided to investigate the situation. While being very careful not to awaken anybody I started to climb the hill keeping my head and the rest of my body as close to the ground as I possibly could. As soon as my head cleared the top of the hill I wanted to shout from joy. It was a tank and it was American! Not only that, there was a column of American tanks extending as far as I could see up to a bend in the road. I clearly recognized the American star on the side of the closest tank. Thank God it was not a Hackenkreutz or a Swastika on a German tank.

We were clearly in a war zone. The first tank in the column had its turret turning slowly from side to side checking the terrain for the possible appearance of German defenders. The question for me was, "How should we surrender to the Americans?" Freedom for us appeared to be so close and yet we had to be very careful.

I deliberately moved backwards very slowly to avoid possible detection and slid down the hill on my behind to share the wonderful news with the others. It was easy to wake everybody up. To explain the problem without creating panic among the more excitable ladies was another matter!

The oldest and tallest lady in the bunch proposed the solution to this dilemma. She was probably six feet tall, or so it seemed to me at the time. She said, "Maciej run quickly to the woods and bring me a long stick." Without asking any questions I immediately obeyed. I brought her the straightest stick I could find, about four or five feet in length. She said, "Fine, thank you," as she grabbed the stick, put it down on the ground next to her while continuing to look through her belongings. The mystery was quickly solved. She pulled out from one of her bags a pair of white, very long panties and said for everyone's benefit, "This will be our surrender flag." She proceeded to turn around, proudly displaying her beautifully embroidered lingerie. Since she had a large frame, this was probably the largest "flag" any of the women could provide.

The next command from her was, "I will go first and you climb the hill behind me. On the double!"

I grabbed my dog, stuck him under my jacket and started to climb the hill. Mother was behind me. The tall lady was a little ahead of the two of us. The rest of the surrender party followed the leader. It wasn't long before my Chihuahua was able to jump out from under my jacket as my body was so close to the ground and started to run ahead of everybody. I desperately tried to catch him but without success. Soon he reached the top of the hill and looked back at us as if we were too slow.

What the soldiers in the first American tank saw was a little dog, a tall woman carrying a white, strangely shaped "flag" on a stick above her head and behind her a group of women and children. When I got to the top of the hill, the tank was slowing down and came to a complete stop. Then, the turret slowly opened. Shortly, the second tank had stopped, then the third and so on.

Since I was the only one in our group that spoke any English, I felt it was my responsibility to talk to the tank crew. By the time I got close to the tank, the head of one of the American soldiers popped out of the hatch on the turret. The first thing I said was, "We are from Poland. Thank you for liberating us." The soldier, with a smile from one ear to the other, yelled out, "I am

Polish too, I am from Chicago and my name is Frank." Then he shouted to his companions inside the tank, "They must be hungry, let's give them some food." In an instant we were literally showered with Hershey chocolate bars and K-rations. Finally, we were free!

An American tank used during WWII like the ones which carried the soldiers who liberated Mat Sikorski and the rest of the people with him.

Epilogue

The second Armored Division tanks of the 9th U.S. Army soon departed, heading for the river Elbe and then, as the soldiers whom I talked to had hoped, the liberation of Berlin. Unfortunately, their advance was stopped shortly thereafter by a decision made at the highest level of the Allied Command. The capturing of Berlin was to be the domain of the Soviet Army. This decision presented problems for a large number of Poles who survived the war and were now in Germany. They did not wish to return to Communist Poland. About 500,000 Polish citizens emigrated to England alone, including my future wife, Barbara, with her parents.

With the emotional departure of our liberators and best wishes all around, we promptly returned to our temporary "factory home" in Hameln after obtaining the verbal assurance that the American infantry would soon follow the heavy armor. Indeed, the next day the first American Army soldiers arrived in a jeep. They told us, after a short visit, that we would soon be moved to better living quarters, which was very welcome news for all of us.

All this happened on April 5, 1944, even before the official surrender of Germany to the Allies. On May 7, 1945, General Dwight D. Eisenhower announced the unconditional surrender of the Third Reich to the United States, England, and Russia at Allied headquarters in Reims, France. The Second World War in Europe had finally come to an end! As promised, our entire group of women with children was relocated to another part of town to an apartment building, under the auspices of the American occupation forces. All over Western Germany large camps were organized for displaced persons (those who opted not to return to Poland) to house, feed and expedite their emigration to different countries.

Now comes the hardest part for me to write about. My mother and I were hoping and praying that my father would survive his stay in the Nazi concentration camp in Germany. However, it was not to be! We knew he had our address since my mother and I received two letters from him when he was in the Sachsenhausen concentration camp. However, he never came to join us when the war ended. My mother, in desperation, wrote a letter to my uncle Wacław Kwiatkowski, my father's brother-in-law. My mother requested in her letter that he search for someone who may have survived the camp and knew something about my father's fate. Two men went to see my uncle as a result of his newspaper ads and radio announcements.

They testified that he was murdered in the camp in January of 1945 by a lethal injection of phenol (carbolic acid) through his chest wall directly into his heart, which caused sudden death. His body was subsequently cremated in the camp crematorium. This horrible news made my mother and me decide that we would not return to Warsaw, but instead, stay in the West.

This was the third time that a major, irreversible, upheaval took place in my life. First, was the Warsaw Uprising. Standing with Enia under my arm in front of our burning home, I could only pray that my life would not end at age 15. The second defining moment was when my father was marched off with the other men, under heavy guard as if they were some kind of criminals, to the Sachsenhausen concentration camp. From now on my mother and I would have to fend for ourselves without my father's love and support! And now here was the third blow, getting the news from Poland that my father would never return! The city of Warsaw was in ruins.

The City of Warsaw was almost as badly destroyed during the Warsaw uprising as was the Warsaw ghetto one and a half years earlier. About 700,000 Warsaw inhabitants were killed during the fighting and the rest were taken to various concentration camps, or to Germany for forced labor under various degrees of severity. Very few people were able to escape the forced exodus and remain in Poland.

I was 16 years old by then and needed to finish high school. There would be no admission to a university without a high school diploma. What were we to do? Fortunately, our future would hold opportunities, which we could not begin to imagine. Since my mother was a schoolteacher by profession, she found a niche for herself teaching children in the refugee camp where we were living at the time. We'd heard a rumor that a Polish high school under British administration was opening in another part of Germany. I immediately applied and was admitted. Hurrah! I was so happy with the new avenue that became open to me. The only unknown seemed to be our hoped-for emigration to the United States. I was quite concerned that I, personally, might have difficulty being admitted to the U.S.A. because of my congenital heart defect. I felt fine, however, and was now not as prone to the frequent respiratory sickness I experienced in Warsaw.

Lucky me! Right after my graduation from high school in June of 1947 at age 18, I returned to the displaced persons camp in Rehden, Germany, where my mother then resided. A few days later, four other boys and I received an invitation to go to Spain and pursue university education in any discipline we desired. All expenses were to be paid by a charitable organization formed in Spain called, "Obra Católica de Asistencia Universitaria" (Catholic Students' Relief

Organization). This was a college scholarship program. It was a wonderful offer, but very scary for me at the same time. I would have to leave my mother and my dog Enia in Germany and live alone in Madrid. The consolation was that my cousin who was two years my senior, was also interested in taking advantage of this unusual offer.

In February of 1948, I arrived in Spain with a pretty thorough knowledge of Spanish since we had a five-month stay in France while waiting for a Spanish visa to be issued. With the help of a Polish/French dictionary and a French book to study Spanish, "L'Espagnole Sans Peine," which I bought in Paris, I had a good beginning in learning both French and Spanish. Latin, which I had to study for six long years in order to graduate from the polish high school, (which I hated with a passion since I thought it to be a dead language), undoubtedly helped me to acquire fluency in Spanish in a relatively short time. I studied electromechanical engineering at ICAI, "Instituto Católico de Artes e Industrias" in Madrid, Spain for one year, and then transferred to the University of Madrid, where I took up physics for an additional two years.

All was going well for me. The teachers were fabulous and my time was spent mostly on studying, writing letters to mother—always inquiring about Enia—and before going to bed spending an hour or so in the chapel, located in the same building. To take a breather from bookwork, I would occasionally help other students to sing Spanish songs to the señoritas over the dormitory telephone. This last activity has contributed to my enduring love for Latin music to this day!

Suddenly, I became worried about Enia because my mother stopped mentioning the dog in her letters. After a long silence she finally admitted that my pet Enia was killed by someone in the camp and purportedly eaten. I feel terrible about writing about this and in such an explicit manner. However, I feel that I owe the truth to the reader of my story since Enia played such an important part in it! I also believe that it is highly unlikely that my mother would have made up the details of this event. She would never allow herself to be insensitive to my feelings. It seems that what is normally considered cruelty by some, may not be viewed in the same manner by others. Their consciences may have been hardened by hunger and the horrific crimes that they witnessed and the hardships they endured.

I am so grateful to God that although I had to face some frightening circumstances during the war, I was never personally beaten or subjected to Nazi brutality of any kind. Millions suffered terribly. This included being starved, tortured and killed, including my dear father. Eating a domestic animal in times of hunger such as during the Warsaw Uprising, I understand, was not a rare event. To have this happen after the war in a displaced persons camp was most unfortunate and revolting to me. This is a sad ending to the story of Enia.

About two years after my departure for Spain, my mother was able to immigrate to America. She was 50 years old when she went to New York and was able to experience more than four decades of life in freedom and comfort, passing away at age 93 in Atlanta, Georgia. First she lived in the New York area in her sponsor's home, taking care of their son who had a birth defect. Later she found a position as the housekeeper in a Polish Catholic Parish on the north side of Chicago. This gave her the opportunity to speak Polish before she could improve her English, and also to prepare the documents for my immigration to America.

Fortunately, we were able to live in close proximity for the rest of her life. She enjoyed many years of peaceful retirement in excellent health. She was able to cook and care for herself until a few months before her death. I am sure this was due in part to her regimen of regular exercise, which at first included following televised programs and then miles of daily walking. She outlasted everyone when it came to house and yard work. Recovery from a breast cancer operation was easier for someone in such great shape both physically and mentally. My mother maintained a sharp mind, no doubt kept active through constant reading and participation in her retirement home's enrichment programs. She was famous for her strong-willed positive spirit. Her greatest joy was being with our family. She cherished every card and gift received and gave memorable gifts to her grandsons. They were impressed to no end that in her 80's she would show off by disco dancing and going on the wild rides at the local theme park!

I came to America on an Italian ship called the "Vulcania," which I boarded in Gibraltar. From Madrid I took a train to Algeciras, Spain and then a ferry across the bay to the harbor. I'll never forget the beautiful, warm afternoon I spent in Gibraltar where I had my first taste of the United States in the form of an ice cold Coca-Cola! It tasted heavenly! Oh, what a sight! I was sipping my Coke and in the background I saw the beautiful, tastefully painted houses with tiny, painstakingly kept gardens rising up the Rock of Gibraltar. Above was the exquisite blueness of the sky and to my right was the somewhat darker blue of the Mediterranean Sea.

Sometime during the night, we entered the Atlantic Ocean. The sea became a little choppy and I woke up feeling queasiness in my stomach. I decided to go and have breakfast to still my queasy stomach rather than waiting for a bigger sign of seasickness. I was so happy to be sailing to America and looking forward to seeing my mother that I decided to celebrate the event by ordering seven sunny-side-up eggs. I repeated this celebration every morning until we reached the Statue of Liberty and the New York harbor. My poor cousin, who was sailing with me on the same ship with his Spanish wife and an infant son suffered greatly from seasickness. Fortunately, I never did!

The first sight on land that I remember after leaving New York harbor was a huge poster for Camel cigarettes. An enormous cloud of smoke was actually coming out of the painted man's mouth on the billboard! Another powerful first impression of America was the deafening sound of vehicular traffic. I hailed a taxi to take me to the Grand Central Station and the train for Chicago, where my mother was waiting for me. In spite of my hard work in Madrid to learn English prior to my departure to America, I wasn't being understood by the locals. It is possible that the culprit was my "British accent," which I acquired by memorizing the contents of a Linguaphone course on the English language, consisting of a number of long playing phonograph records. This was sent to me by my uncle Jan Sikorski in London. Another possibility was that the New York cabbie knew even less English than I did!

What a joy it was to see my mother upon arriving

in Chicago! We had so much to say to each other. We had four years of catching up to do! I left Germany for Spain in 1947 and arrived in Chicago in the autumn of 1951. Now I had one more language and three years of university study under my belt. Very soon I got a job as an electro-mechanical draftsman at a manufacturing company in Chicago. This allowed me the opportunity to practice American English and also, (with the help of a curriculum advisor from the Illinois Institute of Technology) prepare to continue my university studies. I earned my B.S. degree in Physics in 1955 and decided to do graduate work.

In 1956 I met Barbara, my future wife, and subsequently married her in January of 1957. Interestingly, my wife has the same first name, Basia (a diminutive of Barbara in Polish) as the girl I wanted to become, with God's help, when I was little! (When God answers our prayers it is often much later and in a different way than we thought.) We met at a dance in a Polish restaurant in Chicago called "Patria" in Latin and "Homeland" in English. Basia was also born in Poland and, after a stay in England with her parents, came to the USA. In those days after WWII, Chicago was literally the largest Polish city in the world with a population of Polish-speaking people of more than half a million. Warsaw, the capital of Poland, was completely obliterated during the Warsaw Uprising in

1944. Also in 1957, we had our first son, Tom.

In that same year, I became a U.S. citizen and officially changed my name from the Polish "Maciej" to "Mathew." Please note that my "Mathew" is spelled with one rather than two "t"s. I did this because I wanted to exercise, as a new citizen of the United States, my freedom to be different. I have regretted this decision ever since because my first name is often misspelled!

In 1959 a scientist from the Bell Telephone Laboratories in Murray Hill, New Jersey became interested in my research work and as soon as I received my Master's Degree from Illinois Tech, I joined the Mechanics Research Department there. We moved to Summit, New Jersey. My mother and my wife's parents also moved there so that we could live close to each other. It was also in New Jersey that my wife gave birth to two more sons, whom we named Mark and Chris.

I enjoyed my work at Bell Labs very much; however, my attempts to study for my Ph.D. degree, which I desperately wanted to earn (before I died), were not successful for lack of proximity to a university where I could pursue my additional graduate work. In 1965 we moved to Atlanta, where I was employed at the Georgia Institute of Technology. I was hired by my old professor from Illinois Tech to do research in the Physical Sciences Division of the Engineering Experiment Station.

I started taking courses in the department of metallurgy and everything looked promising. Then, at the beginning of 1968, I started feeling particularly tired after work and my headaches were starting earlier and earlier in the afternoon. I needed bed rest for 2-3 hours after returning home from work. My physician suggested that I go to see Dr. John Kirklin at the University Hospital in Birmingham, Alabama for an evaluation. Dr. Kirklin had the reputation of being the foremost cardiac surgeon not only nationally, but also worldwide, specializing in congenital heart defects. I felt he would be the best person to help me. I knew all of my life that I had a bad heart, but the present symptoms alerted me that it was time to act.

I was only 39 years old at the time, but I felt like an invalid. Other men could mow the lawn in front of their houses, but not I. The fatigue I felt was overwhelming, even if I attempted to lift a relatively light object. After my week long evaluation in the hospital, Dr. Kirklin told my wife and me, "If you let me operate on you, there is a 98% chance that the operation will be successful; however, if you wait any longer, the damage done to your lungs will be irreversible." Of course, I said yes. He sewed a woven Dacron patch over the hole I had in my heart since birth. The operation went very well and it allowed me to continue my life much stronger than ever before. For the next three years I was able to procure contracts in the field of biomedical research and felt great that I could contribute to other people's well being. Now, almost 37 years later, I am able to share my WWII memories with the reader.

My graduate studies were impeded more and more by an increasing need to be constantly searching for research contracts, which involved a lot of travel. I was finally able to fulfill my ambitions, when I was invited to work on my Ph.D. degree in Manchester, England. I was receiving a salary from the University of Manchester and all of the research work was applicable toward my thesis, which was phenomenal! Since I received an educational leave of absence from Georgia Tech, I was able return to there with a substantial increase in salary after I received the degree.

I enjoyed my stay in England very much. The hard part was separation from my family, who remained in America for the period of my work in England. All of this was possible because of the business acumen which my wife demonstrated after she decided to go to work when our youngest son reached the age of 14. She said to me, "I did a good job of feeding four men for 14 years and now I am ready to feed people outside our home while making some extra money." After managing someone else's sandwich shop and having a great time at it, she wanted to have her own. This meant that most of our savings would have to be spent on the purchase of furniture and equipment, so that we would not go into debt. I reluctantly agreed to her proposition, not knowing how good Barbara would be at managing her own shop. For almost thirty years her creation thrived as the landmark lunch place in Norcross, Georgia, just north of Atlanta. Thanks to building this sandwich shop for my wife (which she ingeniously, and accurately, called "The Best Sandwich,") I was able to satisfy my educational ambitions and return to America with a Ph.D. degree in Fiber Physics.

Having my Ph.D. degree, I was later able to become a Fellow in the Oxford Society of Scholars in 1998. The publications that I hope to produce will correspond to my present interests in philosophy, psychology, and physiology in relation to religion and spirituality. This was a change in direction for me. It was research into human nature rather than in the physical sciences.

Retiring early, I decided to leave my work in physics and engineering to the younger generation and concentrate on sharing my life experience with others. My father's legacy of purposeful living through personal accomplishments still reverberates in my consciousness today. I remember how much joy he derived from his work and how he was able to blend his unique talents and creativity with service to others. Whatever new approaches he developed in the art of designing men's suits, he shared with the younger generation through teaching. He was a master craftsman and a devoted mentor. I remember how proud I was of him when he would receive a gift from his listeners at the end of each course. These courses lasted from several weeks to several months. He loved doing it, even though he was never paid.

In 1980 I had the opportunity to return to Poland. My son Mark accompanied me on my first trip back to Warsaw since the war. Walking down the street where I used to live, I was so choked up that if I had been asked a question, I would have broken out crying. I felt for a moment that this was still my town. I wondered why I had been away for so long! And yet this was no longer my town, my family now lived in America. I marveled at how faithfully my old neighborhood had been rebuilt. The only thing that appeared different was the Bristol hotel, across the street from my house. It seemed smaller than I remembered it. I was shorter then, so perhaps this would explain my feeling.

The courtyard where I used to play ball and fly my airplanes was still there. The only difference was that instead of gravel, the square was paved and partially used as a car parking lot. The Tailor's Guild building, where my father used to teach, was renamed after the war as the Textile and Apparel Institute. It had been rebuilt on the same location, only two or three blocks from where we lived. It looked exactly as I remembered it. I was touched to see a plaque next to the entrance with my father's name engraved on it, dedicating the main conference room to his memory. This was a total surprise! Again, I was deeply moved, my throat tightened from emotion and I felt like crying. In the hall, opposite the speakers' podium, was a large portrait of my father as the teacher. To the side of this room was a small lecture hall separated by a cloth partition just like it was before the destruction of the building. Suddenly, a vivid memory surfaced when I stood in this "doorway." As a little boy I used to occasionally watch, in awe, my father teach his class from this position. He was such a great and inspiring speaker! There was also an exhibit in the museum section of the building honoring my father. I revisited Warsaw in the '90s and had opportunities to talk to some of my father's tailor-friends. They said that after so many years his design methods of men's suits are still used in their profession. I also heard that my father was preparing additional changes in design for use in the first automated factory of men's suits in Poland after the war.

From the Institute we went to the vicinity of the Royal Castle, which is located at the edge of the Old Town. In the square there is also a tall column with a statute on top honoring King Sigismund, one of the foremost kings in the history of Poland. A street leading to the "Old Town Square," on which St. John's Cathedral is located, featured a number of jewelry stores. I could not believe what I saw on display: earrings; necklaces; rings; bracelets, all featuring amber as the precious stone. I went back in my memory to the times when, at age nine, I used to collect these on the beach of the Baltic Sea, albeit they were much smaller and covered with barnacles, thus hiding their natural beauty. I was aware at the time that amber stones were valuable, but I had no clue how beautiful they look when used in jewelry. I did not know either, and probably was not interested to know at that time, that amber collected on the shores of the Baltic Sea is purported to be about 45 million years old. These stones were formed from the sap of luscious, pine-like trees that were growing where the country of Sweden is now. Because of their chemical composition and physical properties (specific gravity) similar to water, they were quite light and hence were carried in the ocean waves all the way to the southern shores of the Baltic. I just could not leave these stores until I bought presents for my wife.

Extremely sad memories came back to me when Mark and I were walking down several streets in the city. We found, in many locations, commemorative plaques attached to the walls of buildings, marking the sites of executions of innocent men. These terror tactics, if my memory serves me right, have intensified after the destruction of the Jewish ghetto in May 1943.

As we continued walking, I suddenly realized that I was filled with great sadness and hopelessness. I recalled that this is how I used to feel most of the time during the German occupation. Then the realization came that the Germans were long gone, but unfortunately, my memory bank was still full of wartime experiences that the passage of time had not cured. Perhaps these feelings were accentuated by the fact that in 1980 Poland was still a captive nation. A communist regime was still in power. It was so sad for me to observe long lines of people standing in cold and rainy weather for hours and hours in front of stores that happened to be open. Often they did not know what would be available for them to buy on that day, or whether everything would be sold before they were even able to enter the store.

* * *

Currently, at the age of 76, with the help of a pacemaker, I continue to pursue and facilitate spiritual and emotional growth experiences in different discussion groups. How grateful I am to God for preserving my life to this point where I continue to enjoy living in the "land of the free," protected from the tyranny I endured as a child. Religion and spirituality were always the basis for my life.

America provides an environment where the human

spirit can flourish. The virtue of the USA is respect for life and property. The life-enhancing ideas that are generated in this rich climate spread quickly and lessons from the past are available for future generations to learn.

I see America as an ideal, a beacon of light for the whole world—All races and creeds living together in PEACE!

Mat with sons Chris, Mark, and Tom and wife Barbara

Mat and Barbara Sikorski

Appendix

The country of Poland is known for some of its most famous citizens:

- Pope John Paul II – previous head of the Roman Catholic Church who was born in the city of Kraków.
- Frédéric Chopin – Child prodigy pianist and composer of some of the world's most popular classical music.
- Nicolaus Copernicus – Best known for his development of the theory of the earth as a moving planet. He is considered by many to be the father of modern astronomy.
- Maria (Skłodowska) Curie – Polish-born chemist who was the first woman to receive the Nobel Prize. She is known for her work with radioactivity.
- Lech Wałesa - who led the Solidarity movement of the 1980's, which greatly contributed to the fall of Communism in Europe and free market economy in present-day Poland. He was selected by *Time* Magazine as "Man of the Year" for his impact on history.

The two Poles who distinguished themselves in the history of the United States of America were

Kazimierz (Casimir) Pułaski and Tadeusz (Thaddeus) Kościuszko.

- Casimir Pułaski was born in Poland in 1747. He believed in freedom from foreign intervention and fought bravely for it in Poland. He later came to America and offered his services as a military officer to the Americans, who were fighting for freedom from England. He organized the first American cavalry. George Washington made him a General and gave him the title, "Father of the American Cavalry." General Pułaski died in battle.

- Thaddeus Kościuszko was also born in 1746, also in Poland. He was a Polish patriot and commander of American troops in the Revolutionary War. He was also an honorary citizen of France.

Both Pułaski and Kościuszko are truly heroes of two countries.

The country of Poland is named after a Slavic tribe (the Polanie), who lived in the area more than a thousand years ago. The word means field or plain, which describes the farm and grazing land which is typical of much of this part of Europe. The Slavic people lived off of agriculture. Good soil and an abundance of water played an important role to this end. Fish farming also started early here. Pottery and iron smelting were other specialties. Rome was buying iron from this region.

The first organized statehood in this part of Europe sprang up in the Eighth Century in Moravia, as Moravian Duchy. Saint Cyril and Methodius brought Christianity to Southern Poland and the rest of Central and Eastern Europe from Greece. This branch of Christianity is known as the Eastern Orthodox Rite.

Perhaps the most significant date in Polish history is the year 966 A.D. That year, Mieszko, a major political leader, bowing to the influence of his Catholic Bohemian wife, Dobra, was baptized and brought his territory with its people into the Roman Catholic Church.

In 1384, Jadwiga, the youngest daughter of King Louis of Anjou, became Queen of Poland at age ten. She married the thirty-year-old Grand Duke Jagiełło, the ruler of the Pagan Lithuania. Two years later he sought to Christianize and safeguard his country against the enemies to the east and the Teutonic Order to the west. By marrying Jadwiga and converting to the Catholic Church, he achieved his objective and at the same time provided Poland with a new dynasty. He became the King of Poland and established the Jagellonian dynasty. This step was mutually beneficial because it strengthened both nations against the common Teutonic threat. The dynasty ruled the country for nearly two centuries. The Polish empire reached its height during the 1500's, when it covered a large part of Central and Eastern Europe, including Belarus and the Ukraine. Poland became the largest country in Europe, extending from the Baltic to the Black Sea.

In July of 1410, one of the major battles of the Middle Ages was fought in the fields near the village of Grünwald (in the Mazurian Lake District of Northern Poland). The decisive victory crowned the Polish-Lithuanian armed alliance and led to the joining of the two countries. The Grand Duke Jagiełło became the king of Poland, an official act of unifying the two countries.

Poland's economic prosperity in the mid-15th and 16th centuries contributed to the blossoming of a golden age of Polish culture. In this period the Cracow University (also called Jagiellonian) was established, one of the first universities founded in Europe. Also Nicolaus Copernicus (Mikołaj Kopernik) was making his contributions to astronomy at this time.

The 17th century was marked by multiple wars with Sweden, Russia and Turkey. The king of Sweden invaded Poland in 1655. In several months, the Swedish armies occupied much territory. The Jasna Góra Monastery in Częstochowa, which had been turned into a fortified bastion, withstood the Swedish onslaught and since then became the symbol of national resistance. After three years of bitter struggle, the Swedes were driven from Poland.

One of the major contributions in history to the defense of Europe from foreign ideologies was in the battle of Vienna, Austria, on November 12, 1683. Vienna was under attack by the Turkish forces of the Ottoman Empire. When the siege of Vienna started, specially trained Turkish commandoes were digging a tunnel toward the central square of the city for an attack, thus circumventing the town fortifications. During a prolonged battle between opposing forces outside the city walls, a new "weapon" was used against the enemy. The Polish king Jan Sobieski III moved in with his famous 20,000-strong contingent of Husars (also called the Winged Cavalry) through a passage in the woods, deemed impassable, attacked a side of the Turkish encampment and defeated the Turks. Part of the armor of the Winged Cavalry consisted of metal plates, loosely attached to the wing structure. As the horse galloped, these plates vibrated in the wind giving off a tremendous, loud noise. The Turkish horses were not accustomed to hearing such sounds, panicked, threw off their riders and ran off into the distance. This victory prevented Europe from being overrun and effectively stopped the expansion of the Ottoman Empire.

Poland underwent thorough and positive internal changes in the 18th century. The progress was based on a new educational system and democratic reforms. The three powerful neighbors of Poland: Austria, Prussia and Russia considered these democratic reforms a threat to their national stability since they were absolute monarchies. When in 1791 the Polish parliament voted on the famous Third of May Constitution, the first in Europe, and second only in the world (after the U.S.), it was too much to bear for the neighbors. Within 25 years Poland was partitioned between the three powers, none of them alone being able to achieve the defeat of Poland.

After 100 plus years of partition, Poland became free again in 1918, after WWI. This was also the time of the Bolshevik revolution in Russia. When the Bolsheviks started an offensive against Western Europe, Polish armed forces immediately engaged them militarily. In 1920, in the battle for Warsaw, the Bolshevik army was practically destroyed and subsequently retreated eastward from the Polish territory. The plans for the conquest of Western Europe were thus abandoned.

An interesting sideline of the battle of Warsaw is that my father-in-law, Nicefor Dąbrowiecki, was personally involved in this campaign under Marshal Józef Piłsudski, the Commander-in-Chief.

Poland enjoyed only 11 years of freedom between the years 1918 and 1939. The recovery of the nation in almost all aspects of life was most spectacular. I was born in 1929, in the middle of the period of national independence, enjoying the fruits of peace and freedom under the loving care of my parents.

On September 1, 1939, Germany invaded Poland with Hitler's armies. WWII had started. During the five and a half years of conflict, Poland suffered greatly. One out of six Polish citizens were killed or went missing during the war reducing the population of Poland from 36 to 30 million at the end of the war. Six million European Jews, half of whom were Polish citizens, and about one million ethnic Poles lost their lives in the Nazi concentration/extermination camps. In addition, Russians, Gypsies, Jehovah's Witnesses and other "undesirables" (according to the Germans) met the same fate. This was about eleven million people, in all.